# APOSTLES' CREED

I believe in God, the Father almighty,
  creator of heaven and earth.

I believe in Jesus Christ, his only Son, our Lord.
  He was conceived by the power of the Holy Spirit
    and born of the virgin Mary.
  He suffered under Pontius Pilate,
    was crucified, died, and was buried.
  He descended to the dead.
  On the third day he rose again.
  He ascended into heaven,
    and is seated at the right hand of the Father.
  He will come again to judge the living and the dead.

I believe in the Holy Spirit,
  the holy catholic Church,
  the communion of saints,
  the forgiveness of sins,
  the resurrection of the body,
  and the life everlasting. Amen

# WHAT CHRISTIANS

HANS SCHWARZ

Fortress Press    Philadelphia

# BELIEVE

Translated by the author from *Verstehen wir das Glaubensbekenntnis noch?*
© 1987 Verlag Herder Freiburg im Breisgau.

**Library of Congress Cataloging-in-Publication Data**

Schwarz, Hans, 1939–
    What Christians believe.

    Translation of: Verstehen wir das Glaubensbekenntnis
noch?
    1. Apostles' Creed.  2. Theology, Doctrinal—
Popular works.  I. Title.
BT993.2.S3913  1987      238'.11      86–45923
ISBN 0–8006–1959–5

2665L86   Printed in the United States of America   1–1959

# CONTENTS

# PREFACE

What do Christians believe? Can we believe it? There is much ignorance about the Christian faith concerning both its content and how to articulate the faith today. Quite often we assume that this or that has to be believed. When we inquire further, however, we discover that many of these items of faith have never been accepted as dogma in any of the major churches and that these alleged doctrines are understood in ways contrary to those of most respected Christian theologians.

The following reflections on the Apostles' Creed are designed to remove some of these misunderstandings of the content of faith by providing an overview of the basics of the Christian faith. The task of providing an overview is relatively simple, since in most of Western Christendom the Apostles' Creed has become the normative expression of the Christian faith. The second task, however, is more difficult: How can these basics of the Christian faith be understood today in such a way that they are still convincing to us, without allowing us to ignore our knowledge about ourselves and the universe around us? The following reflections attempt to present the Christian faith in tune with today's language and with sensitivity to today's issues. If we can help the reader to rethink the Christian faith anew, then our task has not been in vain.

At this point I would like to thank Bärbel Berger and Barbara Fischer, who helped type the manuscript, Craig Nessan, who offered much appreciated criticism and help with stylistic improvements, and Russell Kleckley, who assisted with proofreading. I would like to dedicate this book to Hans and Krista as they make their transition from childlike faith to adult belief.

# INTRODUCTION TO
# THE APOSTLES' CREED

The Apostles' Creed is familiar to most people who participate with some regularity in Christian worship services. But quite often the most well-known items of our faith are accepted without considering what they entail.

In form and content the Apostles' Creed dates back to the Roman Creed, which was already attested to in Rome in the second century A.D. It has always had its place in the baptismal service. The one to be baptized or, in the case of infant baptism, the parents and godparents, were asked about their faith in the triune God: "Do you believe in God the Father? Do you believe in Jesus Christ? Do you believe in the Holy Spirit?" To each of these questions they answered, reciting part of the Apostles' Creed and thus professing their faith in God the Father, the Son, and the Holy Spirit. In the West the existence of this Creed had become a matter of fact, and only relatively late was it discovered to be only a creed of the West and not a creed in a strictly ecumenical, worldwide sense. In Eastern churches, the Nicene Creed, promulgated in A.D. 325 at the Council of Nicea and enlarged at the First Council of Constantinople in A.D. 381, assumed a position similar to that of the Apostles' Creed in the Western tradition.

The so-called Nicene-Constantinopolitan Creed was formulated because the church saw that the true Godhead and the true humanity of Jesus Christ were endangered. This indicates one of the basic intentions of a creed. A creed is formulated, not simply because one feels like it or because one would like to summarize the faith in a

9

brief way that is easy to memorize, but because one is aware that one's faith is threatened by others. Creeds are formulated against perversions and distortions of the faith by others. This basic intention of a creed came to the fore a mere fifty years ago in the so-called Barmen Declaration of 1934. Barmen opposed the messianic national socialist ideology of the Third Reich, an ideology in which people were made to greet each other with the confession "Heil Hitler" (salvation through Hitler). Against that ideology, the Barmen Declaration of the Confessing Christian church in Germany stated in an unmistakable way that faith in Jesus Christ is the only source of revelation and salvation for Christians.

There is still another point to a creed. A creed does not confess everything one can believe, but only what is central to the faith and from which other areas of the faith can be unfolded. For instance, in the Apostles' Creed we hear nothing about Jesus' miracles or his proclamation. We also hear nothing about God having liberated Israel from bondage in Egypt and having led the chosen people to the promised land, though we believe these items too. A creed is always characterized by its concentration on the essentials at the core of the faith.

Another point must be mentioned. Although a creed often starts with the words "I believe," it is not an individual confession. The creed's function as a baptismal confession already indicates that through this confession one is connected with all those who confess the same faith. A creed signals the unity of those who confess their common Christian faith with the same words. Yet, even as we reflect here so matter-of-factly about confessing the faith, we cannot overlook the fact that in many ways this faith has lost its persuasiveness.

# WHAT CHRISTIANS BELIEVE

# 1 | BETWEEN SUPERSTITION AND UNBELIEF

*"I believe . . ."*

When we consider the first two words of the Creed—"I believe"—we also know that as children of modernity we are used to *seeing* instead of believing. "Seeing is believing," we hear in today's fact-centered world. This means that faith is threatened by faithlessness. Yet, modernity could not do away with faith completely. The emergence of many sects, cults, and other semireligious groups indicates that, from the perspective of the Christian faith, faith is also threatened by superstition. But what is the situation of our own faith?

## FAITH IN A TIME OF SKEPTICISM

In 1957 the sociologist Helmut Schelsky labeled his contemporaries "the Skeptic Generation," in a book by the same title. Schelsky stated that young people are "deeply convinced of a helplessness in planning against the large political and social power constellations." This feeling of helplessness and skepticism seems to have reemerged today. As average citizens we have no way of influencing the mighty power constellations that determine our lives. We have become skeptical of those who high-handedly decide matters of politics and economics that touch all our lives. This feeling of helplessness emerges not only because each person has only one vote in our democratic system, but even more because there is no way of changing things drastically even when we do elect a different government. Certainly the names and the parties change, but the feeling of helplessness remains. Transregional interests and international powers dictate much that touches us, much against which we cannot defend ourselves. So there is only one alternative. Either we go into the streets and protest, a reaction that may have already been taken into consideration by those who make the big decisions, or we resign ourselves and withdraw to the private sphere, attempting to live as well as we can because things simply cannot be changed.

This feeling of helplessness and powerlessness does not immediately change once we encounter the Christian faith. Because we have been continuously confronted with the limits that are imposed in our lives, it is difficult for us to imagine how this faith could help us transcend these restrictions. We also wonder why we should believe all these things that the Christian faith tells us are essential. Is it not better to order our lives according to what is factually given? Amidst this skeptical mood and engendered by this kind of resignation, a strange phenomenon becomes clear: While many people think that our traditional faith is largely meaningless and while many others propose that everyone can believe whatever he or she wants to believe, all of us are conditioned to *believe* in that which is factual. We are convinced that what we see on the news has really happened. But we do not know whether this is actually *all* that happened. Similarly, when we read in the newspaper about a specific event, we are convinced that it actually took place. Usually, however, we are unable to check things out. We collect our knowledge on the basis of faith: the more we hear about or read about something, the truer it must be. This is exactly the method the advertising world employs to convince us. The more often a certain commercial appears on television and the better the product looks, the more we are convinced that we ought to use the product. But the best reporter and the most conscientious journalist can present only part of the picture and even this part is already colored by their own interests and by the expectations of others.

In some closed societies, where information is not freely obtainable, people know that they cannot trust the written word or the information presented on television. Thus, the citizens begin to read between the lines. Even when they do this, however, the information is not more trustworthy and does not present a more objective picture of reality. Even if we are convinced that seeing is believing and that we only believe facts, we cannot circumvent the fact that we must believe and we must trust. Trust is a basic structure of human existence.

## TRUST IS BASIC TO HUMAN EXISTENCE

The feeling of helplessness against those in power that often irritates us as adults is something that we naturally take for granted in the case of infants. As humans we are born helpless. From the first breath we are dependent on other people. At first there is instinctive bonding between mother and child, which gradually gives way to a more conscious bond. A child needs specific fixed points on which it can rely and which it can trust so that its development can proceed without complications. If the people to whom a child relates are frequently interchanged, the child's emotional and physical development may be impaired. When a child enters school, it is once again dependent on people it can trust. One often hears that poor teachers whom a child thinks it cannot trust or who have little interest in their students can make school a miserable experience for the child. As a child grows, the ties to the parents become weaker and faith in their authority diminishes. But the fading authorities of childhood are at once replaced by others. At first the teacher is the final word, but soon teachers are replaced by friends or by a group. Even as adults we cannot live without ties and without someone we can trust. Perhaps we rediscover our parents as persons we can trust; perhaps our focus of trust becomes the woman or man with whom we are willing to venture a life together; or perhaps it is a friend or a colleague at work. We need somebody with whom we can share our life.

The more experience we gain, however, the more we realize that trusting others frequently leads to disappointment. We have all had a friend whom we thought we could trust unconditionally but who disappointed us. We may learn that others found out what we had shared with this friend in strictest confidence. Often the unreliability of friends has also been disappointing in other ways. As long as we do well we have many friends who love to share the limelight with us. But once we are in need and must depend on friends, these friends are quickly gone. The trust we felt in them was simply misplaced. It

is not by accident that Martin Luther's explanation of the fourth peti-
tion of the Lord's Prayer asks, "What does our daily bread mean?"
and answers, "Good friends, truthful neighbors . . ."

Because of the dialogical structure of our personhood, we depend
on others on both good and bad days. We must continuously dare to
approach people and to open ourselves to them even if we are repeatedly disappointed. This disappointment is why many people grow
bitter and shut themselves off from the world. But we can only do this
for a short time without damaging ourselves. Then we must dare to
turn anew toward our neighbor and toward the world. If, however,
our life-experience shows that our trust is frequently betrayed, is not
our turning to another person simply masochism, some kind of self-
destructive mood in which we relish the rejection or disappointment?
No, because we notice a basic dilemma in our existence: Our trust
can never reach its end and goal in the realm of the finite. Only by
trusting the infinite can our trust find its meaning.

## THE INFINITE AND
## OUR TRUST IN THE FINITE

I once heard one of my colleagues ask another colleague: "How
can you exist in this world with your almost boundless trust and your
almost unlimited goodness?" The answer was very simple: "Because I
have experienced in my own life this unlimited goodness and this
boundless trust." Martin Luther thought along similar lines when he
stated in his lectures on the prophet Isaiah: "Those who have no faith
and take refuge in human help will fall and perish."

As finite beings we cannot protect ourselves against every conceiv-
able misfortune. Therefore we are always dependent on a certain
measure of trust. This trust has its limits in the limitations of the
object of our trust. Our trust is always limited, and if we are obliv-
ious to this, it will be misused. In his *Commentary on Galatians* of
1535 Martin Luther said: "The Christian faith always looks toward
Christ; it is not centered on anything else but Christ alone who has
overcome sin and death and who has brought justice, salvation,
and eternal life." This faith or trust that we Christians place in Christ
is quite different from our trust in other people. The faith made possible here is founded in Jesus Christ, and Christ has shown himself to

be infinitely trustworthy. As Luther noted, Christ has overcome sin and death and has brought justice, salvation, and eternal life. These are accomplishments that we are unable to achieve on our own. Therefore Christ has authorized himself as the one who has overcome the limitations of human life and has opened for us the dimension of the infinite and eternal life.

God's infinite goodness, which shows itself to us in Jesus Christ, enables us to turn to other people. It should not surprise us that Christians reach out to others who are in need. We may think here of Mother Theresa working among the outcasts in the slums of Calcutta or of Albert Schweitzer working as a missionary doctor in the tropical forests of central Africa. In them and in many others we can see how the experience of the gracious turning of God toward us is transformed into our turning to other human beings.

Faith, then, does not mean that we can enumerate all the things we believe. Nor is faith synonymous with a credulity in which we close our eyes and rush blindly into anything that might be offered to us. Faith stems from the experience that there is something beyond the fragmentation of this life which is worthy of our trust. Faith is sustained by God's infinite love, which enables us to live in this world and turns our attention to the needs of the world. Faith leads to the acknowledgment that even in the midst of immense political and social pressures we have not lost the future. Faith means trusting in the one in front of whose throne all powers have to bend their knees, whether they are in heaven or on earth. When we confess our Christian faith anew every Sunday, this is not a sign that we have lost touch with this world. On the contrary, the "I believe" that we jointly confess makes sense out of this world. Without a faith that transcends the limitations of this transitory world, fragmentation and insufficiency would have the final word. But the "I believe" is a strong promise that all the question marks of this world will find meaning and fulfillment in God.

# 2 | PROFESSING A PERSONAL GOD

*"... in God, the Father ..."*

Though we may still use the phrase "God the Father," it is no longer commonplace that we believe in a personal God. While there have always been people who doubted God's existence, most of them did not think that God was totally superfluous. They only doubted whether a certain god was still trustworthy. When this happened they would scout the many other gods until they found one on whom they thought they could rely. Therefore the psalmist could rightly say that only the fool says in his heart, "There is no God" (Psalm 14). For the psalmist it was natural to believe in God. Only somebody out of his mind, a fool, could doubt God's existence. Today we would no longer argue in this way. Often the most thoughtful people assume that they can dispense with God's existence.

## DOUBTING GOD'S EXISTENCE

Ludwig Feuerbach is usually considered to have been the first strong proponent of modern doubt in God's existence. He thought that God could be explained as our attempt to secure ourselves in the world. He reduced God to a human phenomenon, claiming that human beings alone could be religious because only human beings possess self-awareness. If we had no desires, Feuerbach claimed, we would have no religions and no God. God is the expression of our desires and our wishes, which we project on the screen of our consciousness as fantasy which we then believe to be real. The human desire for something beyond itself is therefore nothing but the desire for human perfection. Because we experience our own imperfection, God assumes more and more perfect features.

In a radical way Karl Marx brought the ideas of Feuerbach to their logical conclusion by making God into a projection of our desires and employing this idea as a central focus of his social revolutionary thesis. If we abolish God and the hereafter, we can devote our time to this world and realize our dreams here and now. Religion, therefore, is declared an opiate for the people. When we take away from the people the illusionary hope for a better world beyond, then they can transform this world into a garden of paradise. This is the Marxist thesis. Of course, we can question whether the Marxist-Leninist theories have really been successful in changing this world into a better place. But it would not be wise to begin our criticism of the Marxist-Leninist theories with this point because their proponents could easily rationalize their lack of success by claiming that too many people still believe in God. This potential apology indicates something important. In many socialist countries the idea of God has been officially declared nonsense for several generations, and even though this propaganda has been supported by governmental and societal pressures, the idea of God has not been easily extinguished. It has not collapsed. On the contrary, especially among younger people in socialist countries, there seems to be an increasing interest in religious questions. The spirits that should not have existed at all have still not been tamed.

Doubt in God also emerges from a different direction. At the beginning of the last century the French mathematician and astronomer Pierre Laplace presented to Napoleon his five-volume work on celestial mechanics. With great interest the French chief-of-state asked Laplace where in his system was there a place for God. Proudly, the mathematician replied: "Sir, I do not need this hypothesis." Though Laplace was not an atheist, here it was publicly announced for the first time that God has no place in a scientific system. In a similar way Charles Darwin once mused: "I would like to give God more room in my system. But the more I talk about divine providence the more uncertain this system becomes scientifically." There is nothing intrinsically wrong with a hypothetical atheism that distinguishes strictly between books on God and books on mathematics, physics, chemistry, and history. But within two centuries this hypothetical atheism has turned into an atheism in principle. At the close of the last century the German biologist and philosopher Ernst Haeckel expressed this eloquently in his book *The Riddles of the Universe,* in which he claimed that God is a gaseous vertebrate. God must be a vertebrate because we claim that God has personlike features. Yet at the same time, God must be gaseous because God is withdrawn from our investigation. With his definition Haeckel wanted to render God impossible on both a theoretical level and a practical level.

The exercise of doubt in God's existence has moved from the professor's desk and the researcher's laboratory into our everyday life. Though "In God we trust" is printed on our greenbacks and though many of us belong to Christian congregations, most of us basically live our everyday lives without any consideration of God. Most people need God only in times of crisis when they are otherwise unable to find a solution. Even practicing Christians tend to relegate God to the Sunday morning service. In doing this, our vision of God becomes hazy. God is reduced to a fringe phenomenon in our lives, and hardly gives us new impulses for daily life. Most of us still live according to moral precepts that somehow are connected with the Christian God. But even so, we are hardly aware of an active God. As Dietrich Bonhoeffer once said, we live as if God did not exist. We should ask ourselves, however, whether we have become happier people through this eclipse of God. Many of us cannot even answer this question because we cannot remember how it was before. Many have lived whole lives in the eclipse of God. But when we carefully look at our lives, we notice rather quickly that the place which has been traditionally occupied by God or which rightly belongs to God has not remained empty. The adventure with God has simply been carried out under a different name.

## ADVENTURE WITH GOD

Each of us has something to which our heart clings, something so important that it influences our decisions. It may be an ideology such as the American dream; it may be the family for which we live or the job in which we find self-gratification. Something always serves as the absolute according to which we order our lives and behind which everything else is secondary. The crucial question is whether these primary reference points really carry us through the currents of life. What happens, for instance, when our children leave the nest or our marriage partner dies? What happens if we lose our job, even though we always had been told that we were irreplaceable? Or what happens if we discover that the ideology which we followed is only a fragmentary truth that we ourselves have absolutized? All the reference points that act as substitutes for God and with which we try to give order to our lives can carry us only so far. Sooner or later, we discern their limitations and are forced to look for other reference points, which in turn also prove to have limitations. So we stagger from one reference point to another without ever really being oriented. In many ways we resemble blind people trying to tell one another which way to go.

Our experiences of the failure of such limited points of orientation lead us time and time again to ask whether there is an alternate orientation and a final truth. The quest for God as the ultimate foundation that can endow our penultimacy with meaning has not lost its significance today. Of course, even when God is introduced, the venture quality of life does not disappear. When we rely on God, we cannot eliminate the risk factor even though many people live under the illusion that as soon as God enters the picture everything will turn out "just fine." At the same time, however, venturing our lives with God does not mean that we are stepping out on thin ice. Three examples from the history of God's people help to illustrate this.

Abraham was already up in years when God spoke to him: "Go from your country and your kindred and your father's house to the land that I will show you" (Gen. 12:1). We are not informed whether Abraham had prior experiences with God. It appears in the text as though out of the blue that God told him: "Venture with me." Abraham could only rely on the promise: "I will make of you a great nation, and I will bless you, and make your name great" (Gen. 12:2). Together with his family and another relative, Abraham ventured with God. Trusting in God's promise, he left home and moved toward the unknown. As we read in the following verses and chapters, Abraham was not spared the ups and downs of life. There were anxieties and disappointments for him. More than once he questioned what the future would bring. But it was important and comforting for Abraham that God promised not to leave him alone. God was true to this promise even though that did not always seem to be so. At the end of his life the blessing that had been promised to Abraham took on a visible dimension. He became the ancestor of a great people.

Let us take Moses as our second example. He had fled from Egypt because he could no longer face the oppression of his people and had killed an Egyptian. Among the nomadic hill tribes he found a wife and took up life as a shepherd. Suddenly God encountered him and made this command: "I will send you to Pharaoh that you may bring forth my people, the sons of Israel, out of Egypt" (Exod. 3:10). Moses had all kinds of excuses why it was not possible for him to go to Egypt. But there was no way out. God left him no way of escape. Finally Moses assumed his task, and after difficult negotiations he led his people out of Egypt and wandered with them for years through the desert. Often Moses asked himself whether he had done the right thing when he ventured with God. This venture seemed much too big for him, and even the Israelites occasionally doubted Moses' leadership abilities. Yet at the end of his life, after all the ups and downs, the disappointments, pleasures, and hardships, he was allowed to see the promised land. He knew that the venture had paid off, that all the drudgery had not been in vain.

As a third example, we may look at the life of Dietrich Bonhoeffer. He was from a middle-class family. His father had been a university professor, and he himself was destined to become professor of theology. But the Third Reich thwarted his plans. Dietrich Bonhoeffer could not remain silent in the face of Nazi tyranny. Therefore he joined the Confessing church. On a trip to the United States he was offered a position at Union Theological Seminary in New York so that he could escape from his difficulties with the Nazi regime. Yet, against strong advice from his American friends, he decided to return to Germany. He wanted to be an upright witness of God during this time of trial and contribute his part to the rebuilding of Germany at the end of the Nazi tyranny. But things happened differently. Because of his connections to the resistance movement against Hitler, he was imprisoned and finally sent to a concentration camp. On one of the last days of the war he was murdered in a little village near the Czech border. One could say that his venture with God did not pay off, but such a conclusion would be wrong. Until the very last hour of his life he was an inspiration for others. Since his death he has remained more influential than almost any other contemporary theologian, both for ordinary Christian believers and for academic theologians. He became what he always wanted to be, a witness to a gracious God.

When we talk about God we must realize that life with God is a venture. But for our Christian faith in God another point is equally important. Christians do not simply believe in some ultimate principle, in a world architect, or a first unmoved mover. They go one decisive step beyond such philosophical faith and turn to the God who is known to us as the Father of Jesus Christ.

## GOD'S GOODNESS

The God of mercy disclosed to us as the Father of Jesus Christ should not be mistaken for a patriarch who authoritatively determines what must be done and whom we must obey unless we want to face unpleasant consequences. Nor should God be mistaken for the one to whom the German poet Friedrich Schiller referred when he said: "Above the firmament a gracious father dwells." God does not pull the ropes of history from somewhere up there and then complacently look down on us earthlings.

As we can see throughout Judeo-Christian history, God enters our history. God suffers with us, is happy with us, warns us, and is even anxious about us. To this God nothing human is unknown. God knows the high points and the depths of our life. Because God knows us so well, God does not abandon us. In the prayer that we share in common, Jesus taught us that we can address God as a child addresses a parent—in trust, confidence, and dedication. When we see that God always cares about us anew and that it is through the graciousness of God that we are still alive, it would be absolutely wrong to conclude that God is a softie or somewhat senile. God does not depend on us. To God we are only little specks in an immense universe. Yet amazingly, God shows interest in us, goes after us, and does not abandon us. God's history with us human beings is the history of a great invitation.

This does not mean that Christians are spared doubts about God's existence. Even for us, living with God remains an adventure, but along the way we also receive ever anew God's undeserved goodness. Martin Luther expressed this in an enduring way as he reflected on the medieval situation out of which he came. He wrote in the explanation of the first article of the Apostles' Creed:

> I believe that God has created me and all that exists; that he has given me and still sustains my body and soul, all my limbs and senses, my reason and all the faculties of my mind, together with goods and clothing, house and home, family and property; that he provides me daily and abundantly with all the necessities of life, protects me from all danger, and preserves me from all evil. All this he does out of his pure, fatherly and divine goodness and mercy, without any merit or worthiness on my part. For all of this I am bound to thank, praise, serve and obey him. This is most certainly true.

Luther expressed here something that should still make us think today. Everything that we take for granted we owe ultimately to God's undeserved goodness. In a time in which many things that once seemed to be "essential ingredients" of life have become questionable again, this confession of a personal God can encourage us to go beyond taking for granted our richly blessed lives and to once again perceive them as God's undeserved gift. Perhaps our lives would then also recover some of the dignity that is often lost in the pace of everyday living.

# 3 | POWERLESSNESS AND OMNIPOTENCE

*". . . almighty . . ."*

In the Middle Ages people suffered under the notion of a powerful God. Today, in contrast, we suffer from the perception of God's powerlessness. A Jewish theologian once wrote: "If God existed, he would have never permitted Auschwitz to happen. If he had permitted it, then we would have to strip him of his divine office." A Protestant theologian expressed the same sentiment with these words:

> The God, who is accused of allowing innocent people to suffer is God Almighty, the King, the Father, and Ruler of the world. Modernity is justified when it accuses him, and all theological trickery to silence this criticism through the authoritative claim that God wants us to be silent because it is only his privilege to ask questions, can not extinguish the truth of the question concerning God Almighty. If one does not want to silence these questions or repress them religiously, they lead to the thronement of a theistically understood God.

## SUFFERING GOD'S OMNIPOTENCE

Some twenty years ago, when I worked in a factory to pay my way through school, I realized that suffering from the perception of God's powerlessness can lead to God's dethronement. My closest colleague at work was an older man whose kindness I appreciated. One day he realized that I was studying theology, and he confessed that he did not believe in God. To my surprised question, "Why?" he answered: "When I look around and see all the cruelty and injustice in today's world, I cannot believe in God." Many people despair over the discrepancy between the idea on the one hand, that God ought to exist and the realization, on the other hand, that so many ungodly and anti-godly powers are present in our world. In bewilderment they ask: "Why doesn't God clean up and create order in this world and establish justice and peace?"

These questions threaten our personal faith. Last summer, when I was suddenly struck with pleurisy, I asked my doctor what might have been its cause. He answered: "I don't know. But the questions 'Why me?' and 'Why now?' are asked me by almost every patient who is struck with a severe illness." A teacher of theology once said: "A human being is shaken up most when he or she knows that it could have been otherwise." The questions why *I* had to get sick, or why *my* marriage partner had to become unfaithful, or why *my* children had to turn against me are difficult for most people.

The Book of Job is devoted to these questions. We read that Job was a prosperous farmer who was liked by everybody. He had sons and daughters and enjoyed a happy family life. But suddenly, so we read, everything went wrong. His farmhands were slain by hostile tribes, his herds were stolen, and his children perished through natural disaster. He himself was struck by illness. Finally even his wife turned against him, saying: "In the face of this, what is your piety good for? Where is your God who helps you?" The three friends who had remained by him were not much help either. They too wondered: "Something must have been wrong with you. Otherwise God would not punish you so much." But against the advice of his wife and probably also against the way we would have acted, Job did not turn away from God. Still, he could not understand why all of this had happened. Finally he turned to God and asked: "Why did you do this to me? Are you not unjust?"

We might object that, in claiming that he did not deserve his misfortune, Job was rather daring before God. But at the same time we must concede that Job had always been an upright person and had not done anything wrong to anyone. So it is easy for us to side with Job. How can God, who is introduced here as God Almighty, play such havoc with a human life? How can God permit the suffering, injustice, and pain that resulted? When God finally responded, according to the Book of Job, God put Job in his place, saying that Job was only a tiny speck in the universe, who was unable to judge God's power and sovereignty. Therefore he had been presumptuous in questioning God's actions. Many of us would not be satisfied with such a response and would not accept it as an answer. The question remains: Why doesn't God's omnipotence eliminate injustice, suffering, and pain in this world?

Perhaps we should also consider the end of the Book of Job to get a more complete picture of God's ways: "And the Lord blessed the latter days of Job more than his beginning" and "Job died, an old man, and full of days" (Job 42:12, 17). This sounds like the happy ending to a Hollywood movie. But if we simply were to follow this interpretation, we would have grossly misunderstood the intention of the book. The Book of Job does not give us a clear answer to the why-question. An answer probably cannot be given in this world. But the ending of Job shows us that, seen from its final outcome, Job's history with God does not end in disappointment. While in the darkness of each individual day Job might not have seen God and even less understood God, the end was not disappointment but fulfillment.

Our own faith in God Almighty must also face the challenges of everyday life. We cannot simply believe in God by closing our eyes. Such a faith would be equated with the sacrifice of our intellect, as sheer credulity. Perhaps we should recall the struggles of Martin Luther. He himself did not suffer from the notion of the powerlessness of God; on the contrary, he suffered under God's power. If God is as the Bible tells us, Luther argued, then nothing is hidden from God, and we must account to God for every minute of our lives. Weak as we are, however, we could never endure the confrontation with such a God. This God would immediately condemn us and there would be no hope for us beyond death. Luther's frightening realization of God's majesty and omnipotence created an almost total sense of despair and led him to a complete reconsideration of his life.

## A NEW OUTLOOK ON LIFE

When Luther discovered that Jesus shows us a God who cares for us as an earthly parent does, he realized that this God could not be a threatening and angry tyrant who mercilessly demands accountability for our lives. Nor could this be the kind of God who uses power like a demon to make us suffer or to deceive us. Luther recognized that ultimately God always wants our salvation. Therefore God gave us the promise that, regardless of what happens in this world, grace will finally triumph in our lives. Since Luther discovered this gracious God through reading the Bible, he emphasized that we must cling to God's Word, for it is not a condemning and punishing Word but a Word of hope and guidance.

Luther, however, realized that the God who wants to be with us must also be an almighty God whose Word cannot be thwarted and whose plans cannot be hindered. That God and God alone has the power to save was vital for Luther. If God has given us promises, God also must have the power to endow them with reality. One of Luther's most incisive theological treatises, *On the Bondage of Will*, deals with God's power. In this work Luther emphasized that omnipotence is the supreme principle for God's activity.

It is certainly not by accident that the two passages in the Bible which state that nothing is impossible for God are concerned with God's activity for our salvation. The first time we hear of God's omnipotence is when Abraham's wife Sarah smiles in disbelief as she hears God's promise that in her advanced age she will give birth to an heir (Gen. 18:14). Again, when it was announced to Mary that she would give birth to the savior of the world (Luke 1:37), we hear that nothing is impossible for God. God's omnipotence is never used frivolously or arbitrarily, but to ensure that God's promises are endowed with truth.

For Luther, God's omnipotence was decisive. God alone can endow promises with reality, and there is nothing remaining for us to contribute to our salvation. Luther recognized that whenever we cooperate in something the outcome becomes uncertain because of our limited energies and endurance. But if God alone brings about the promised goal of a new world and a renewed humanity, we can rest assured that God's promissory word will not return empty. It is a word that affects history and will change the world.

Luther was not, however, a naive optimist. He knew about the dark side of history. He also faced up to some tough questions: If

God is indeed almighty, why is there so much evil in this world and why does God not change demonic people through whom inexpressible suffering is brought into the world? Luther did not know the answer to these questions. He confessed that these things are part of God's mystery, which we cannot fathom. Luther emphasized, however, that we are not to remain with an unfathomable and mysterious God. Instead, we are to "flee" to the revealed will of God, which tells us that behind all darkness and ambiguity there lies a future for us. Luther told us that we should cling to God's gracious will as revealed in Christ and to God's promissory word. Then we will realize that God is indeed trustworthy.

## GOD'S TRUSTWORTHINESS

Dietrich Bonhoeffer's notes from his prison cell in Nazi Germany, published under the title *Letters and Papers from Prison*, contain two statements that powerfully illustrate the experience of God's trustworthiness. First, we read in Bonhoeffer's notes: "God does not give us everything we want, but he does fulfill all his promises." Bonhoeffer knows that God's omnipotence has limits for us. Often we desire that something in this world should be changed, and we ask God to do that. God listens to all our desires but does not comply with all of them. God alone decides what will be translated into reality. Sometimes we are unhappy if things do not change the way we want them to. But we do not know what lies ahead of us—what the next year, the next week, or even the next day will bring. Many fairy tales warn us of the consequences of having all our wishes brought to realization. In our ignorance of the future and our often thoughtless spontaneity, we would frequently cause more disaster than good. Therefore it is beneficial for us that God alone, from whom nothing is hidden, outlines the future for us.

Bonhoeffer also states: "I believe that God is not a timeless fate, but that he expects and responds to sincere prayers and responsible actions." God is not a timeless fate that can be compared to the so-called laws of nature or some kind of otherworldly referee who impartially metes out good and evil. God's power can never be separated from God's fatherliness toward us. God wants to have a dialogue with us and does not want us to lead our lives in oblivion to

God's presence. But such a dialogue shrinks to a monologue if the other side does not respond. Therefore, our prayers, which we have often reduced to the form of intercessory prayers, make sense only if they reach God Almighty. God then responds to our prayers and grants blessings to benevolent actions.

Prayers cannot replace action, however. Martin Luther insists that only in rare exceptions does God act without mediators. Usually, ordinary people serve as the masks behind which God acts so that it appears as though we ourselves do everything, while ultimately it is God who accomplishes everything. Luther encourages us to become God's arms, feet, and hands to remake the world more into what God intended it to be. When our intercessory prayers are accepted by God, seldom does something occur in a way in which it could not naturally occur. For instance, when a prayer is accepted that we successfully pass an exam or that we recover from an illness, it would be strange if this could not also be due to our careful preparation or the skill of the doctors. But these natural causes should not obscure the fact that behind everything is ultimately the will of God Almighty.

At times God's will may become enigmatic and unfathomable. But we cannot remain fixed upon God's unfathomable majesty without suffering in our Christian life. Therefore, we should always look to the place where God's omnipotence becomes intelligible to us and possible to grasp—the place where God became human. God has shown to us in Jesus Christ that there is a promise and a way for us beyond all the ups and downs in our life. In graciously coming to us God has given us an aid through which we can bear the enigmatic character of our life. Since Christ has overcome the world, we do not need to be afraid of it. We can accept our own place in life responsibly and trust God's gracious power.

# 4 | CREATION AND SCIENTIFIC KNOWLEDGE

*". . . creator of heaven and earth."*

The German philosopher Martin Heidegger once said that "no other epoch has accumulated so great and so varied a store of knowledge concerning man as the present one. . . . But also, no epoch is less sure of its knowledge of what man is than the present one." Contained in this statement is the entire problem of how we can believe in God as the Creator of the world without compromising scientific knowledge.

We know so much about the development of the universe, of the animal kingdom, and of humanity that it becomes more and more difficult to comprehensively grasp all the continuously expanding specialized knowledge. The wealth of specific information seems to defy the development of a satisfying and well-grounded overview. Some people tend to absolutize individual facts and then make generalized confessions with amazing self-assurance: "Humanity is only a special form of the primates" or "God created the world in seven days." Often such ideological absolutism results in ideological warfare, as is being waged once again between creationists and evolutionists. One side vilifies the position of the other as "materialistic atheism" or else as "scientifically ignorant fundamentalism." When we ask, however, how the Bible regards the relation between God's creation and our natural knowledge, we learn that the confession of God as the Creator of heaven and earth does not serve to absolutize individual facts.

For the Israelite faith, belief in God the Creator never had a very high priority. It was much more important to the Israelites that God had a special relationship to them, that they were the chosen people. God had chosen to identify with specific events in their history, such as the exodus from Egypt or the events at Mt. Sinai, and on the basis of these events the Lord was the creator and the guarantor of their history. Since Israel was also confronted with the creation myths of its neighbors, it gradually clarified the role of its God in creation. Israel affirmed that the God whom it had experienced in its history as a people, as clans, and as individuals, was none other than the Creator of the whole world. God as the Creator, therefore, was no independent object of faith but was derived from Israel's previous confession. Because God had shaped Israel's history, the Israelites concluded that God must also have initiated that history and would also bring about its fulfillment. As we will see, however, belief in God the Creator can also be derived from our natural knowledge of the world.

## GOD THE CREATOR
## AND OUR NATURAL KNOWLEDGE

The creation account on the first page of the Bible starts with the well-known words: "In the beginning God created heaven and earth." This confession of God the Creator is then expanded in the following verses. Though the details give us sufficient insight into how the Israelites at that time perceived the world around them, it would be wrong to interpret this confession in God the Creator of heaven and earth as a scientific world view comparable to the scientific knowledge of today. Rather, with this confession at the beginning of the Bible two ideas were made unmistakably clear. First, God is the Creator of the whole world. Second, the world itself is not divine but created by God. Both statements were quite controversial at that time and have remained controversial until today.

In virtually all religions there are creation myths that tell us how a creator god or several gods have created the world in a laborious but finally successful way. In the environs of Israel there were a number of such creation myths, but the Israelites were never attracted to them. Since their God was the only God who mattered, no other gods could have been necessary to create the world. It was also incompatible with their experience that God should have created the world in a laborious way after a hard, long struggle against all the obstructing powers, as they heard from the creation myths of their neighbors. Their experience with God was so overwhelming that they confessed their God to be the one who had created the whole world with incomparable sovereignty and ease. God did not need other gods, nor did God need preexisting items as "construction materials." The world was created, so to speak, out of nothingness, putting into existence that which had not previously existed.

While the Israelites were convinced that God had created everything "good" and that humanity was destined to function on earth as God's representative, created in God's likeness, it was foreign to them to think that there was anything in the world that could have divine qualities. Though the Israelites were not safe from spiritual mistakes, they realized that only God the Creator could be divine. Everything created, while sanctioned and authorized by God, was without divine quality. When we compare the neighboring religions of Israel, then we understand the implications of this claim. To say that God made the sun, the moon, and the stars was tantamount to a rejection of the alleged divinity of these sidereal powers.

Since God was understood to be the Creator of the world, the created could be stripped of its divine qualities. It was possible to explore the world and take it into human service. But in our time the desacralization of the world has assumed such thoroughgoing dimensions that many people are even tempted to remove God from the world. Yet we simply are not able to do without some kind of ultimacy. As soon as God the Creator is removed as the foundation of the world, the world itself begins to assume absolute features. As a consequence, people have proclaimed the absoluteness of matter and the existence of ironclad natural laws. Some have even asserted that the world is endowed with eternal qualities and that everything in it runs according to unchangeable laws. Creation eventually assumed absolute features from which humanity has tried to derive a sense of security. But we have discovered that it was wrong to endow creation with absolute features. The absoluteness of matter has been dissolved by its transformation into energy, and natural laws have shown that they are derived from experience. Recognizing the relativity of these building blocks has increased our sense of disorientation.

Perhaps at this point we should recall the philosopher Immanuel Kant, who once claimed that the starry heaven above us and the moral law within us are the best witnesses to God's existence. Even the British astronomer and skeptic Fred Hoyle once stated that through the increase of our knowledge the world has become, not more plausible, but even more enigmatic. For him, as for many others, the existence of some kind of higher being has become an almost unavoidable conclusion. It would be wrong, however, to assume that the biblical faith in God the Creator can be equated with the idea that there is a higher being who once gave origin and direction to the world. For the Israelites of the Old Testament and for the Christians of the New Testament, faith in God the Creator is not a theory about the past but rather a hope for the future.

## NEW HOPE FOR THE FUTURE

In the nineteenth century God found no place in what became a materialistic world view. The mood surrounding this change was one of optimism and self-assurance. For many people the world had assumed eternal features. From Charles Darwin they thought they had learned that through the ongoing evolutionary process humanity could strive to entirely new heights. Of course the individual human being had no hope for the future since the individual was considered to be only matter, but the future of humanity as a whole was painted in bright colors. In an enlightened age that was turned toward the future, it was thought at the end of the nineteenth century that even war had become the archaic relic of a savage age. It no longer had a place in enlightened humanity. In peaceful competition humanity would develop to ever higher spheres. But, as we know, things went differently.

Through two devastating world wars and almost continuous regional wars, faith that an eternal peace can be humanly created has been shaken drastically and lastingly. Today's peace movement, with proponents in almost every country, is not born out of a naive optimism but results from a basic anxiety that through our own failure the world could be ruined forever. Even nature does not give us great hopes for the future. The law of entropy tells us that our world has no eternal future ahead of it. Everything will come to a standstill once the different energy levels have attained a universal equilibrium. Many scientists tell us that this process cannot be changed and that at some point we will encounter a rundown world in which life is virtually impossible. This second law of thermodynamics, the law of entropy, has been unfamiliar to most of us.

Acid rain, dying forests, the destruction of the environment through technology, and the depletion of nonrenewable resources confront us with an endangered future. Though we should always have known it, only gradually do we now realize that unhindered growth is only possible in cancerous cells. But such cells in turn destroy sound tissue. In a finite world we cannot expand steadily. Sooner or later we will see the limits of what the earth can bear. Even if we were as frugal as possible, sooner or later an end would come to this earth. In knowing more and more about nature, we become ever more convinced that all our plans and hopes face the limit of life and these plans will perish together with life itself.

The Israelites were realistic about nature. They realized the finitude of human life and this world. For instance, we read in Psalm 90: "The years of our life are threescore and ten, or even by reason of strength fourscore; yet their span is but toil and trouble; they are soon gone, and we fly away" (Ps. 90:10). Yet this psalm does not just express the finitude of human life. At the very beginning the psalmist states: "Lord, thou hast been our dwelling place in all generations. Before the mountains were brought forth, or ever thou hadst formed the earth and the world, from everlasting to everlasting thou art God" (Ps. 90:1-2). Israel was certain that the God who had created the world and everything in it would also provide us with a new future beyond the finitude of this world.

The same word used to denote the divine creative activity at the beginning was also used to indicate God's redemptive creativity at the end time. The one who gave a beginning to this world can also break through the cycle of growth and decay in which we find ourselves. The Israelites became convinced that God can give this world a new beginning. Belief in creation in this way is central for any hope that there is something to look for beyond this perishable world. But perhaps such hope is simply a projection of our desires and wishes, which has been skillfully connected with faith in God the Creator. In assessing the gravity of this objection we must go beyond the Old Testament. We will see that faith in God the Creator is also the actual content of the Christian faith.

## PRESSING ON TOWARD A NEW CREATION

The New Testament is convinced that our future is not simply still to come but has already proleptically occurred in the Christ event. For instance, we sing in an Advent song:

> Wake, awake, for night is flying,
> the watchmen on the heights are crying;
> awake, Jerusalem, at last.

That which shall give hope to the whole world has already occurred in Christ. Therefore Paul reminds his fellow-Christians that they are a new creation, that the old has passed away and something new has appeared. Now, Paul was no naive utopian. He realized that the world continues to follow its usual course, that the stronger overpowers the weaker, and that death awaits us at the end of life. But he also realized that these biological and historical givens are not all-determinative for us. Because Jesus Christ has shown us a new future beyond death, there is hope beyond the world's finitude. Therefore, Paul contrasted the first, old Adam to Jesus as the new Adam. For Paul, the resurrection of Jesus was rightly understood as God's *new* creative act through which the world has been given a *new* direction, even as it had to some extent already been anticipated. Therefore Paul wrote to the congregation in Rome:

> I consider that the sufferings of this present time are not worth comparing with the glory that is to be revealed to us. For the creation waits with eager longing for the revealing of the sons of God; for the creation was subjected to futility, not of its own will but by the will of him who subjected it in hope; because the creation itself will be set free from its bondage to decay and obtain the glorious liberty of the children of God. We know that the whole creation has been groaning in travail together until now; and not only the creation, but we ourselves, who have the first fruits of the Spirit, groan inwardly as we wait for adoption as sons, the redemption of our bodies (Rom. 8:18–23).

This new quality of life will some day be revealed. It is the content of the Christian hope that then all the darkness, ambiguity, and fragmentation of this world will be forever overcome.

Without belief in God the Creator, who gives our lives a new direction, we are subjected to the limits of this world. Therefore, it was important for Martin Luther to know that God does not act like a human artisan who creates something and then abandons it. God continuously stays with the creation. God not only began it but also completes it. The confession of God the Creator is not a theory about the beginning of the world. It is a confession of the One of whom we sing:

Eternal ruler of the ceaseless round
Of circling planets singing on their way,
Guiding the nations from the night profound
Into the glory of the perfect day:
Rule in our hearts that we may live anew
Guided and strengthened and upheld by you.

# 5 | JESUS CHRIST—SAVIOR, HERO, OR FAILURE?

*"I believe in Jesus Christ, his only Son, our Lord."*

In exploring the first article of the Apostles' Creed, which centers on God, we noticed several times that we cannot talk about God without considering Jesus Christ. In this century the quest for God has been pursued with new intensity. Yet this quest always seems to direct us back to the person of Christ, lest God become an anemic and hazy figure.

It is common knowledge that the center of the Christian faith is Jesus Christ. We notice this when we simply compare the length of the three articles of the Apostles' Creed. The second article, dealing with Jesus Christ, is by far the longest. Often talk about God virtually disappears behind our emphasis on Jesus Christ, but we should never forget that Jesus Christ himself represents God and points to God. Any assertion about Christ must ultimately be one about God. Here, however, another danger emerges, that is, that Jesus be pushed out of the center because he is considered merely as one who points to God but is not himself worthy of being honored as God. If we draw such a conclusion, we join the ranks of those who affirm Jesus as no more than the founder of the Christian religion.

## THE FOUNDER OF
## THE CHRISTIAN RELIGION

Without a doubt, we simply cannot think of the Christian faith without considering the person of Jesus of Nazareth. In this way we can justify the assertion that Jesus of Nazareth has founded the

Christian faith. He can be seen in analogy to people such as Siddhartha Gautama, who founded Buddhism; Mohammed, the prophet of Islam; and Lao Tse, the founder of Taoism. These seminal persons have changed the course of history and have left a lasting imprint on the human mind. Millions of people have received from them their values and world views.

We may want to penetrate further and ask how deep are the values mediated by religion. Are not wars waged even today in the name of religion, in places like Northern Ireland and Lebanon? Although these conflicts are frequently identified with specific religions, we should not overlook the fact that these hostilities are ultimately not religious but political. Political power is often clothed in religious terms because the various contenders for political power themselves belong to different religions.

Even so, we must admit that the history of many religions has been tainted by violent conflicts. These conflicts, however, are not grounded in an animosity inherent in any specific religion but rather in the zealous engagement of religious believers who did not want others to succumb to error. It is ironic that those who escaped from religious persecution to the shores of the "New World" initially succumbed to the same kind of intolerance toward one another as that from which they had fled in the "Old World." Only gradually was religious tolerance established.

When we consider human dignity and the infinite value of the individual, we find that these phenomena are inseparably connected with the Christian faith, just as equanimity, patience, and compassion for all living and nonliving beings is associated with Buddhism and the subordination of one's own desires under the ruling will of Allah is connected with Islam. These deeply religious values have made life more bearable and more human.

It would be shortsighted, however, to consider Jesus of Nazareth only as the founder of a new religion. This assessment would contradict the witness of the Christian faith. In contrast to the aforementioned world religions and their founders, the Christian faith confesses Jesus Christ as the object of divine veneration. For a faithful Moslem, Mohammed always remains a prophet, though certainly the most prominent. For a Buddhist there are prayers to Buddha, but they are not addressed to a god, as a Buddhist is quick to point out. Lao Tse, too, is venerated only as a wise teacher. Among Christians, however, the conviction emerged almost immediately that they should not merely promulgate the message of Jesus but that Jesus should become central to the message as the one who is worthy of being proclaimed. The assertion that Jesus is more than the founder of a religion has been found offensive to many people. They ask, "How can a human being who once lived among us on earth be more than a human being?" To consider this objection we must inquire more carefully regarding who Jesus actually was.

### A FIGURE OF HISTORY

Modern historical science has given us two important facts about Jesus of Nazareth. First, through careful study of the available sources and through critical comparison with his contemporaries, Jesus has emerged as an actual historical figure who has passed through the acid test of historical study. The amount of reliable information about Jesus of Nazareth widely surpasses the information about many other historical figures of antiquity. We have much more historically reliable information about Jesus than about Plato or Siddhartha Gautama. Second, beyond these reliable conclusions about the historical figure of Jesus, modern science has also shown us that this information is not sufficient to write a biography of Jesus with all details included. Many of the stories about Jesus presented by the evangelists must be recognized as narratives and not as reports. They were written with the intention of showing how important and significant Jesus is. They are not neutral and unbiased factual reports.

Still today the figure of Jesus fascinates many people, as we can see by the renewed interest in Jesus' Sermon on the Mount. Jesus is often understood as a wisdom teacher who conveys many important insights. Even the Indian statesman Mahatma Gandhi often quoted passages from the New Testament to his fellow Indians to show them how they should lead their lives. In this respect the New Testament is still cherished by many. From it we can learn how to get along with each other, the infinite value of the individual before God, or how to conduct our everyday lives. Frequently the two-fold commandment of love—"You shall love the Lord your God with all your heart, and with all your soul, and with all your mind, and with all your strength" and "You shall love your neighbor as yourself" (Mark 12:30-31)—has been considered the center of the Christian faith. But in so doing we may forget that here Jesus was only quoting two Old Testament passages (Deut. 6:4-5 and Lev. 19:18).

A historical figure—and Jesus is no exception—must always be seen in context. We cannot remove Jesus from his historical context and simply appropriate his sayings without running the risk of misinterpreting them. If we want to transfer an assertion to the present, we must know what it meant in its own time and how its meaning can be mediated to us today. If we consider Jesus of Nazareth as a timeless figure, he loses his roots in the history of Israel. But if we consider Jesus in the context of his history, then another difficulty emerges which Gotthold Ephraim Lessing formulated two hundred years ago in this way: How can an accidental truth of history become a reliable truth of reason?

The broad gulf of two thousand years of history between Jesus and us can hardly be bridged. Jesus was a simple Jew who presumably was brought up in a carpenter's shop. For a few years he was an itinerant preacher in an area smaller than the state of Ohio. He developed a small following until a violent death put a premature end to his life. How can such a person still have significance for us today unless he is taken out of the limitations of his history and transposed into something of eternal value? Such attempts, however, to remove Jesus from history are always tinged by subjectivity.

Albert Schweitzer, medical doctor in Equatorial Africa, interpreter of Johann Sebastian Bach, and New Testament scholar, pointed out at the beginning of this century that each generation creates its own new image of Jesus. In the nineteenth century there was the Jesus of liberal theology and before that the Jesus of the Enlightenment. Today there is the Jesus of liberation theology and the peace movement. Yet a Jesus of our wishes and desires cannot ultimately be reliable. We relativize him when we attempt to exempt him from the relativity of history. Jesus can only become reliable when we recognize that in the particular history that took place in and with him, something emerged that is of significance for us today. The Apostles' Creed affirms the vital significance of Jesus. It calls him Christ, our

Lord, and God's only Son. With these phrases it asserts that he was not just a figure of history who lived nearly two thousand years ago somewhere in a corner of world history. On the contrary, Jesus is the one who shapes history.

## THE AGENT OF HISTORY

If Jesus is regarded as the Christ, then this is not a concession to those who seek to see in Jesus the fulfillment of messianic expectations. Jesus did not establish the messianic kingdom on earth for which some had hoped, and he did not give new splendor to the Jewish nation. Jesus rejected any ethno-political messianic claims and emphasized that his kingdom was not of this world. That Jesus was called the Christ is founded on the fact that Jesus met the messianic expectations in a very unexpected way. The messianic expectations found their fulfillment by transcending the ethnic limitations of Israel. Though some of Jesus' followers did not immediately agree, the recognition soon set in that with Jesus all ethnic limitations had disappeared and he was the Christ, the Messiah, of the whole world.

In Jesus God acted decisively for all humanity. The people were led from a distant God to the God revealed in Jesus Christ. Since God identified with Jesus of Nazareth, this particular Jew was relieved both of his human limitation and of his historical relativity. He became the image and mirror of God in a true sense. When the Christian community confessed Jesus as its Lord, this was not just a polite gesture of showing loyalty. A recognition that Jesus is the Lord excluded allegiance to any other lords. It also meant that one could expect something from Jesus that one could not expect from other people. He is the actual Lord; he is not just a figure in history but its decisive agent.

Through God's presence in Jesus Christ, the destiny of humanity has been changed. We need no longer live distant from God but can realize that God takes us seriously as persons and provides a future for us beyond the limitations of our own history. Martin Luther knew this when, in his explanation of the second article of the Creed, he immediately referred to the existential significance of the Christ event and expounded it in detail. Since Jesus Christ is the one who shapes history, we cannot avoid him. Our future is determined by our relationship to Jesus Christ. In this way we can affirm the words that Jesus speaks in the Gospel of John: "He who sees me sees him who sent me. I have come as light into the world, that whoever believes in me may not remain in darkness" (John 12:45-46).

In the Psalms we read that God said to the king of Israel: "You are my son, today I have begotten you" (Ps. 2:7). This promise has been picked up by Christians in reference to Jesus as the only Son of God. Here the identity goes much further because with the Israelite king it ended with his death. Since Jesus was true to his father throughout his life on earth, God has also identified with him in and beyond death. This was eloquently expressed in an ancient Christian hymn when it said that Jesus "humbled himself and became obedient unto death, even death on a cross. Therefore God has highly exalted him and bestowed on him the name which is above every name, that at the name of Jesus every knee should bow, in heaven and on earth and under the earth, and every tongue confess that Jesus Christ is Lord, to the glory of God the Father" (Phil. 2:8-11). God identified with Jesus to such an extent that a totally new quality of life has emerged, which will be transferred to us. With the destiny of Jesus is connected a hope for all of us. Jesus becomes both a model for our faith and the one from whom our faith gains strength.

As we have seen, the confession of "Jesus Christ, his only Son, our Lord" does include our faith in the founder of a great religion and an impressive figure of history. But important as this may be, it cannot by itself undergird our faith. Only the recognition that Jesus Christ is not just a link in history but one who actually has shaped history and will continue to shape it can give us a reason to trust, and new courage.

# 6 | THE BIRTH OF THE GODHEAD

*"He was conceived by the power of the Holy Spirit and born of the virgin Mary."*

No Christian festival is dearer to our hearts than Christmas. Even in the United States, which takes pride in its traditional separation of church and state, Christmas has become a holiday for virtually everyone. While Christmas is one of the three main Christian festivals (the others being Easter and Pentecost), it has only been positively recognized by the church since the middle of the fourth century. At first, resistance against introducing this festival had been quite strong because it seemed too similar to the pagan custom of celebrating the birthday of kings. Moreover, December 25 is not the original birthday of Christ. Before this date for Christmas had been chosen, the church in the East, for example, had celebrated Epiphany on January 6 as the birthday of Christ. The Orthodox church still maintains this custom.

The origin of the Christmas festival as we know it today is connected with the church of Rome. When the Roman bishop chose December 25 to celebrate the birth of Christ, he may have been motivated by the fact that Emperor Aurelian had designated the same day as the festival of the sun. In this way the bishop wanted to affirm the victory of Christ, the true sun, over the pagan cults.

This polemical character of the Christmas festival has been maintained until today. In our time we must fight the Christmas rush and the sentimentality surrounding the little babe in swaddling clothes lying in the manger in order to realize that it is the human birth of God that is truly at the center of Christmas. When we consider the assertion of the Apostles' Creed, " . . . conceived by the power of the Holy Spirit and born of the virgin Mary," it is easy to overlook the polemical intention of this phrase. First of all, this phrase asserts that Jesus was not some kind of divine-human being.

## JESUS WAS NOT A DIVINE-HUMAN BEING

In Greek mythology there were many sons of gods. Most of them entered human history in coming to the aid of people, but ultimately it was their fate to succumb to the destiny of the world. For instance, Heracles, the son of Zeus, accomplished many heroic deeds. Finally, however, he was put to death by his wife. It was known throughout antiquity that sons of gods could offer only temporary help to humanity. They could not be relied upon forever. This was also known in New Testament times. Similarly today when we elevate people to an almost divine status, whether they are entertainers, sports heroes, or politicians, they may deliver what we expect from them for a while. Eventually, though, their fame declines and we must resort to new heroes and stars.

For the people alive at the beginning of Christianity, the decisive question was whether Jesus too was one of these divine-human beings. If one could answer this question with a yes, one could only expect temporary help from Jesus. Soon his star would decline and other helpers would become necessary. Therefore one should not venture one's life in expecting too much from such a messenger of the gods. For instance, when Paul introduced himself to the congregation in Rome, he wrote to them very clearly that Christ was more than a messenger of God, that Jesus Christ was "designated Son of God in power according to the Spirit of holiness by his resurrection from the dead" (Rom. 1:4). Paul affirmed that the good news which he proclaimed was not just news about another messenger of God but from God's own Son enthroned in power. In the Creed, too, the assertion that Jesus Christ was conceived by the power of the Holy Spirit indicates that Jesus Christ is alive.

In the famous christological and trinitarian controversies of the fourth and fifth centuries, who Jesus Christ really was was carefully examined. It was then decided that it was not sufficient merely to assert that Mary had given birth to the Messiah. There had already been too many messianic figures for such a statement to express adequately the ultimate significance of Jesus. It was more important that Mary was described as the one who had given birth to God. This statement seeks to express that in Jesus Christ God actually assumed human form. In the earlier versions of the Apostles' Creed one still confessed that Jesus "is born from the Holy Spirit and the Virgin Mary" so that the reference to Mary emphasized the human origin of Jesus and not, as was later the case, the divine origin. But even then it was clearly asserted that Jesus Christ was also of divine nature. This coming together of the divine and the human described by the term "virgin birth" is quite often perceived as a stumbling block.

## THE MYSTERY OF THE BIRTH

In the first centuries after Christ the affirmation of the virgin birth was something quite common for most people. A virgin birth was, so to speak, a status symbol. Everybody who had special significance was born by a virgin. Even someone like Alexander the Great, whose biological parents were well-known, was thus said to be born of a virgin. This means that a virgin birth was not always understood as a strictly biological fact but rather was an indication that the person thus born was of special significance. If we were to interpret the confession of the virgin birth of Jesus in a similar way, we would in no way violate the context in which this confession is to be understood and evaluated.

Very early, however, there arose polemics against the virgin birth of Jesus as likewise against many other assertions of the Christian faith. For instance, the early Christian theologian Origen told us of a Platonist named Celsus who claimed that Jesus was not born of a virgin but instead was the result of a relationship between Mary and a Roman mercenary by the name of Panthera. It is also important to note that only two New Testament witnesses, Matthew and Luke, mention the virgin birth. The other two Gospels are silent about the birth of Jesus. In Paul we find only this statement: "When the time had fully come, God sent forth his Son, born of a woman, born under the law" (Gal. 4:4). Concerning this passage, it goes without saying that a woman is not necessarily a virgin. Paul wanted to emphasize the divinity of Jesus when he said that "God sent forth his

Son," and he wanted to point to Jesus' humanity when he wrote that he was "born of a woman, born under the law." This reference in Paul's Letter to the Galatians does not even touch upon the issue of the virgin birth.

Considering the scant historical evidence, we could elevate the virgin birth to a dogmatic principle and assert that by exclusion of the male role the sinlessness of Jesus was maintained. Yet such an assertion gets us into another set of difficulties because it implies that sin comes into the world through the procreative act. This, however, contradicts God's command that calls us to fill the earth and to procreate.

Still another danger arises when one asserts that Jesus must have been born without a human father. It makes it questionable whether or not Jesus actually became a human being at all, since it would mean that Jesus became a human being, not as we did, but only through being born of a virgin. If this were true he would not even have encountered the kind of humanity that we have. Already at birth he would have been different from the way we are and his whole dwelling on earth would actually be a farce.

We should, however, remember at this point that the assertion of Jesus being born of the virgin Mary initially served to affirm that Jesus was indeed a human being and not that he, so to speak, walked two feet above the ground throughout his life. The birth of Jesus reported by Luke took place in a far corner of human civilization, among roughneck shepherds, and in a drafty shed. It does not indicate that Jesus was any better off at birth than we are. On the contrary, with his first breath Jesus experienced what it means not to be among the privileged of this earth.

There is still another way to explain the virgin birth. It is sometimes believed that the woman is always passive and the receiving one, while the man is active and the giving one. In the birth of Jesus the man had to be excluded so that God alone was active and the woman the passive. But when we consider the whole person, we cannot make such a distinction between man and woman. Both man and woman can be active and passive depending on what the life situation demands of them. While in the course of history Mary was often elevated to the devoutly obedient and passive servant of God, we notice that according to Luke even Mary had her doubts about what was to happen to her.

The human birth of God was such an exceptional and improbable event that even the "best" human being, as many people consider Mary to have been, was herself truly amazed. It seems that even with our most ingenious attempts to explain the secret of Jesus' birth we do not make any headway. But the Creed is not really intended to provide a reasonable investigation of what occurred nearly two thousand years ago. Rather, it reflects the confessional realization that Jesus Christ is of twofold origin.

## THE TWOFOLD ORIGIN

The twofold origin of Jesus was one of the most intensely debated theological issues in the history of the church. It took four centuries to gain clarity on two questions: "How is Jesus related to God the Father?" and "How is the human in Jesus related to the divine?" In attempting to find an answer to the first question regarding Jesus' relationship to God, two items had to be excluded: First, it was necessary to affirm that Jesus was not just a son of God but that he was equal to God. Only when he was equal to God could we expect divine help from him. Second, however, Jesus could not become another god next to God the Father. If there are two gods, one easily arrives at a dualism, the belief in a creator god and a redeemer god, and the question remains undecided as to whether the redeemer god will finally prevail. Therefore, the insight confessed in the Nicene-Constantinopolitan Creed was that Jesus Christ is of equal being with the Father and that he is venerated and adored together with the Father. In other words, God the Father has identified with Jesus of Nazareth in such a way that when we worship God the Father we do not neglect the Son and vice versa.

The second question was even more difficult to decide: How are the divine and the human aspects related in Jesus of Nazareth? One could object that this is a speculative question and totally irrelevant for us today. If we agree to this, however, we overlook the fact that theological questions are almost never posed sheerly out of the joy of speculating but are usually derived from a serious existential interest. This is certainly true in this case. The underlying question was whether in Jesus Christ we really encounter God. The church father Irenaeus rightly stated that what God has not assumed, is not redeemed. If God was too good to identify totally with our world, then it is questionable whether our human world will find its way to God. Only the complete presence of God in Jesus Christ can assure us that God desires to be so close to us as to assume community with us. But Jesus of Nazareth must have been a totally *human* being too. If he was only a messenger of God or a being somewhat similar to us humans, then he would always have remained surrounded by a halo and would not have completely identified with us. We would then be left to ourselves and could not hope for unity with God as the goal of our life.

If, however, we meet a human being in Jesus of Nazareth who is at the same time God, then the question emerges how both features can be related to each other in one person. For instance, would Jesus resort to his divine nature to accomplish miracles while his suffering would only be an expression of his human nature? Thoughts like these are quite dangerous. If Jesus could simply resort to his divine nature once things got difficult for him, then he was clearly better off than we are. He was then no human being in the full sense, and he did not identify with us completely. Furthermore, if only his human nature suffered, then the divine did not really live through the depths of our human existence.

At the end of this long struggle to clarify these difficult questions, the church basically did not know any more than it did at the beginning. It did realize, however, that in Jesus the divine and the human aspects can be neither separated nor mixed together; nor can they be brought into some kind of higher unity. Jesus Christ, so the Creed said, was truly human and truly divine. But even the most serious investigations could not tell us how we can rationally perceive this divine-human unity of the person. We return once again to the essential point that has been asserted in the Apostles' Creed: Jesus of Nazareth is of twofold origin. On the one hand, he has been created by the Holy Spirit. God is present in him through the Spirit. On the other hand, Jesus of Nazareth was born by a human being, the virgin Mary. Therefore he is a human being just as we are.

Since the human and the divine are intimately and inseparably connected in Jesus Christ, we can hope that also in our lives we can again be joined with the divine. We are allowed to hope that we can find our way back to the one who, as Augustine said, has created us and who keeps our hearts restless until we rest in him. The incarnation of God has nothing to do with sentimentality about a little babe in swaddling clothes and even less with the hectic Christmas rush. The birth of Christ does, however, contain the promise that we are allowed to find our way back to the one who is our origin, to God, our Creator and our destiny.

# 7 | SOLIDARITY WITH THE WORLD

*"He suffered under Pontius Pilate, was*
*crucified, died, and was buried."*

A brief survey of what we find mentioned in the Apostles' Creed and what we do not find there offers us some surprises. In contrast to the Gospels there is no mention in the Creed of Jesus as a preacher. We also hear nothing of his miracles. Yet quite extensively we hear about Jesus' suffering and death. By mentioning the Roman procurator of Judea, Pontius Pilate, Jesus' suffering is connected with world history. The extensive account of Jesus' suffering and death is certainly no accident but serves strong apologetic interests. Jesus Christ, the Son of God, has shown his solidarity with the world. He did not avoid entanglement with its dire reality. Since Jesus Christ represents God, this also means that God has shown solidarity with the suffering in the world. Yet a suffering Christ who is the actual redeemer of the world somehow offends our sense of propriety. A famous American theologian once declared that Americans would rather worship a Christ without a cross. But we are not alone in this sentiment.

## A CONTRADICTION TO OUR SENSE OF VALUES

Recently I attended a conference at which I met a Hindu from New Delhi, India. He told us in our conference section that a few years ago he had visited Rome. He had seen St. Peter's and the world-renowned Pietà, by Michelangelo. He conceded that the sculpture of the dead Jesus held in the arms of the mourning Mary was an artistic masterpiece. Yet somehow this deceased Jesus remained alien to him, as did the many crosses with the suffering Jesus on them that he saw in Rome. A Buddha, he mentioned, would never have been depicted like that. Buddha died as if he were slipping away into a better beyond, with a smile on his lips and his face relieved that his suffering was over. A suffering Jesus, the Hindu confessed, simply contradicted his idea of a redeemer.

The figure of Buddha is typical for the way salvation is depicted in most other religions. Savior figures usually do not identify themselves with the suffering and death of this world. They want to draw their adherents away from this world and its suffering and lure them to a better beyond.

Even the Jews could not find any sense in the cross of Christ. As Paul stated, the crucified Christ was a stumbling block to them (1 Cor. 1:23). They had hoped that their Messiah would relieve them from the humiliation they suffered under the Roman occupation army. They hoped he would liberate Israel and lead it back to the original splendor of the Davidic kingdom. The Romans too could make no sense of a crucified Christ. This is shown most vividly in a graffito that has been found in the Paedogogium, a training school for court pages, on the Palatine hill in Rome. This graffito shows a young man standing in front of a cross on which there hangs a human figure with the head of an ass. Underneath there is written in Greek: "Alexamenos worships his God." What had been written on the wall by one young man in his scorn indicates what many others also thought of the God of the Christians. A god who allows himself to be crucified is not worthy to be god. He can only be an ass, otherwise he would have used his divine power, humiliated his persecutors, and eliminated his enemies. The adoration of such a god convinced the pagan Romans that these Christians were totally out of their minds.

This negative attitude toward a suffering god has been maintained throughout the centuries. Barely fifty years ago Alfred Rosenberg in his *Myth of the 20th Century*, a book that decisively influenced Nazi ideology, wrote about Christ: "It is his life which is of significance for the Germanic person and not his painful death." Following Friedrich Nietzsche, Alfred Rosenberg saw in the veneration of a suffering

God a portrayal of the Christian servant and slave mentality. Rosenberg did not want to have anything to do with the humble Lamb of God. For him it was the heroic figure of Jesus that was decisive as he showed himself in the cleansing of the temple. The crucifix, which is always connected with this "awful depiction of suffering," only makes sense according to Rosenberg in that it helps the church rule more easily over its devout believers.

We must ask ourselves why in antiquity, in modernity, and in other religions, there is little understanding of a savior who suffers and finally dies. The answer is quite simple: God and the world are seen as incompatible realities. The sentiment rules that a god from whom we may expect salvation must be so superior to this world that he can never completely identify himself with it and its dark sides. For instance, in Gnostic myths the savior leads his adherents from the depth of this world to a new and higher world. Even the true believers feel they do not fit into the world. They renounce the world through asceticism or transcend it through ecstasy. It is not surprising that such a picture of God always borders on projection. Because we long for something absolute beyond the transitoriness of this world, we project our desired salvation above and beyond this world. Yet the Christian faith is vehemently opposed to this kind of projection. According to the Christian faith God does not live in higher spheres, looking down on us and somehow feeling sorry for us. On the contrary, in Jesus Christ God shows solidarity with us.

## GOD'S SOLIDARITY WITH US

In our most recent times it has especially been Latin American liberation theology which has emphasized that God shows solidarity with those who are among the suffering and oppressed in this world. God is not with the strongest guns, as some people still thought a generation ago. Throughout the Judeo-Christian tradition we notice a continued awareness that God is a just God, a God who especially disapproves of social injustice. God is the God about whom Mary sings in the Magnificat in Luke after the announcement of the birth of the Savior:

My soul magnifies the Lord, and my spirit rejoices in God my Savior, for he has regarded the low estate of his handmaiden. For behold, henceforth all generations will call me blessed; for he who is mighty has done great things for me, and holy is his name. And his mercy is on those who fear him from generation to generation. He has shown strength with his arm, he has scattered the proud in the imagination of their hearts, he has put down the mighty from their thrones, and exalted those of low degree; he has filled the hungry with good things, and the rich he has sent empty away. He has helped his servant Israel, in remembrance of his mercy, as he spoke to our fathers, to Abraham and to his posterity forever (Luke 1:46–55).

This early Christian hymn does not only indicate that this unimportant Mary was chosen by God in an indescribable way to give birth to the Messiah. How God is depicted here is much more important. God is shown as being on the side of those who are without power and who are oppressed, and is the one who provides justice and freedom for them. God's solidarity with the poor and the oppressed is shown over and over again in Luke's Gospel. Jesus shows in the parable of the rich man and the poor Lazarus that earthly well-being does not imply that one is blessed by God (Luke 16:19–31). In the same way we hear Jesus saying at the end of the parable of the good Samaritan: "Go and do likewise" (Luke 10:37). Jesus wanted his followers to express solidarity with those who are oppressed and exploited.

The reference in the Creed that Jesus Christ suffered under Pontius Pilate, was crucified, died, and was buried identifies Jesus Christ with the suffering of this world. But it is no exclusive solidarity with a certain class, by which the oppressed would become the new rulers and then rule over those who initially were in power. The solidarity of Jesus Christ encompasses all of humanity. Jesus identifies himself with those who are downtrodden and heavyladen, regardless from where they come.

This all-inclusive solidarity shows that Christ's life and destiny portray the life and destiny of each individual human being. Regardless of our rung on the social ladder and how liberally we are blessed by success, sooner or later each of us will face suffering against which we are ill-prepared. And finally, it is death that awaits each and every one of us. The saying that "the last shirt has no pockets" indicates that we will leave this world as empty-handed as we entered it, regardless of how much luck and happiness we had in this world. If we are blessed by old age and are not taken away earlier through a cruel and unrelenting death, we will notice how our stamina will gradually decrease as we slowly but steadily approach death. Neither makeup nor facelifts nor fitness courses will ultimately help. At best we can slow down the process of decay to which we are all subject, but we cannot eliminate it. This phenomenon of ultimate helplessness, which includes suffering, perishing, and death, was not avoided by Jesus Christ. Even at this point he showed his solidarity.

But how can such a suffering Son of God help us if he too suffered in this world? Are not other religions and other approaches to life superior when they assert that their savior was exempted from transitoriness? Is it not strange that the suffering Son of God finally proved to be so attractive that he has followers all around the globe? Perhaps more is contained in his suffering with the world than we might initially suspect, even though the image of a suffering Christ contradicts our sense of values. The story is told that before a decisive battle against a contender for the rule of the western Roman Empire, the Emperor Constantine had a vision in which he saw a cross and heard a voice saying: "In this sign you will be victorious." The sign of weakness and offense that had prompted a young man on the Palatine to deface the crucified Christ with the head of an ass seems to contain true hope.

## ONLY A SUFFERING GOD CAN HELP US

Of course, one can interpret the cross as a sign of defeat. Martin Luther knew how improbable it is for us to expect anything good from this sign of offense. Just recently it was brought home to me again that through the suffering and dying of Christ a totally new understanding of God is opened up for us. This happened at the previously mentioned conference on God's significance for us today. The conference was divided into several different sections, one on God and women today, another on God and transcendence, and so forth. In some of these sections there were more Buddhists and Hindus than there were Christians. In my section, however, which was on God and the poor and rich nations, there were only two non-Christian representatives, one Hindu and one Moslem. All others were Christians—from Africa, Latin America, Europe, and North America. When I told my research assistant that in my section there had been only two non-Christians, his reply came rather quickly: "This shows that these religions prefer the escape route."

Indeed, there is a decisive difference whether God really identified with this world to bring it to its final completion, or whether God, as most religions suggest, has turned away from the world and leaves it to condemnation and decay. A god who does not actually suffer with this world will more than likely sooner or later exclude us too from sympathy and leave us to ourselves. When Buddha passed away in peace and tranquility, he left only some good ideas about how we can live in peace with nature, with our fellow human beings, and with ourselves. Buddha is rightly understood as a teacher of wisdom, whose doctrines one must follow to obtain eternal bliss.

At the end of the earthly life of Jesus, however, there is no peaceful dying. Instead there is this sigh: "It is accomplished." Jesus did not merely leave us rules for how we could obtain peace with ourselves, with other people, and with the universe. The peace after which we long cannot be attained by us. In its fullness it is something that only God can give us at the end of time. In this present world we have, at most, longer or shorter moments of relief before we turn this world into hell for one another. But the tearing of the curtain in the temple in the front of the Holy of Holies coinciding with Jesus' death, indicates that Jesus provides us once again with access to God. Because of Jesus' death we can live and die in peace with God. God is not a distant God who turns away from this world and its suffering but a God who is close at hand and who suffers with us. What is more, the experience of peace with God also results in peace with other people and with the world in which we live.

That Christians help in many places in the world, through activities such as Bread for the World or Miserior, reflects some of the suffering with others that Christ has shown us in his life and in his death. Though we call some people saints and martyrs, most of us are caught up in self-destructive egotism. But God does not remove us from this world and lead us to another and better world. On the contrary, God sends us time and time again into this world that we might become arms and hands of God, showing sympathy, administering help, and alleviating suffering. God does not abandon this world as we might throw away something that did not turn out well. Solidarity with the world as we encounter it in Jesus' life and death is not an exclusive privilege of the children of God. It must also lead us to become God's followers.

We learn something more when we look at Jesus' suffering and dying. We learn that suffering and death are not God's final word. Since God allows Godself to be drawn into this process, we may rest assured that through suffering with us God will put an end to suffering. The suffering and death of God necessarily entail the overcoming of suffering and death. This is the deepest reason why only a suffering God can help us.

# 8 | CHRIST'S
UNIVERSAL SIGNIFICANCE

*"He descended to the dead."*

The belief in Jesus Christ as the one who descended into the realm of the dead is attested for the first time by a version of the Apostles' Creed that was used in the fourth century in Aquilaea, at that time an important city north of Venice. The version of the Apostles' Creed that we have from second-century Rome did not yet include this phrase. Thus Jesus' descent to the dead is the last addition to the Apostles' Creed.

The reference to Jesus' descent to the dead has often caused misunderstandings. For instance, a few years ago one of my theological teachers suggested to me that liberalism had finally watered down even the Apostles' Creed: where it once said that Jesus Christ descended into hell, now we only confess that he went to the dead. Thus, hell had been eliminated from the Apostles' Creed. I responded by assuring my teacher that these were certainly not liberal trends because the present phrase "he descended to the dead" is much more akin to the original Latin version than the familiar "he descended into hell." This reference can be understood as a further elaboration of what had already been mentioned before in the Creed, namely, that Jesus had actually died. Through death he entered into the reality of all the other dead, into the realm of death. Yet exactly at this point the musings of the early church were aroused. What does it mean that Jesus, who is both divine and human, has actually died? The answer was given in the confession that Jesus Christ went to the dead. In this reference speculation and existential interest are inseparably connected.

## SPECULATION OR EXISTENTIAL INTEREST?

The early Christian community assumed that during the three days between Good Friday and Easter Sunday Jesus was in personal unity with all the dead, that is, in the realm of death. This was his point of deepest humiliation, of utmost helplessness, and most intensive solidarity with us. He was exactly where we all will one day be when, as dead persons, we will be totally reliant on God's grace and compassion.

Though in more recent times Lutherans and Reformed debated whether Christ's descent into the realm of the dead was the deepest point of his humiliation or the beginning of his exaltation, it was soon evident for the early Christian community that Jesus Christ did not wait passively like everybody else for the redeeming help of God. It was argued that since Jesus Christ was truly divine, the divine could not rest inactively for three days. Though it had died together with the human being Jesus of Nazareth, even in the realm of death Jesus' divine nature had to be active. It is easy for us simply to shake our heads at such speculation and affirm that the beyond simply cannot be understood as a continuation of this world. In these reflections the realm of the dead is conceptualized too much like a real geographically localized realm "down there," where Jesus must have dwelled after his death. Such inadequate reasoning almost tends to disqualify the active confession that Jesus Christ went into the realm of the dead. We know all too well that if we penetrate to the interior parts of the earth we reach deeper regions of the earth and not the realm of death.

Beyond these speculative considerations that are difficult for us to accept, there is, however, a manifest existential interest which must be considered. In the first Christian communities, whether Jerusalem, Corinth, or Rome, as we must recall, there were only Christians of the first generation. They had become Christians because they were deeply convinced that only Jesus Christ could show them the way to God and that otherwise it was impossible for them to obtain completion of their lives. This early Christian faith, however, in no way meant that they were egotists who rejoiced in their own salvation without concern as to whether others had equal access to the ultimate future. Quite the opposite! They tried as hard as they could to spread the good news of salvation so that as many as possible could realize its promise.

Nevertheless, the enthusiasm of these early Christians in spreading the Christian faith as far and as wide as possible throughout this world could not solve one problem that bothered them ever more deeply. What would happen to their relatives and ancestors who had been born too early to assent to the good news of Jesus Christ? Were they forever excluded from the immediacy with God? Had they forfeited the completion of their lives beyond death? Through their understanding of Jesus' message, however, one point became increasingly clear to these early Christians: the God who had been revealed in Jesus Christ could not be a narrow-minded God whose main interest was to exclude as many as possible from the kingdom. Hadn't Jesus himself always told them that God's compassion was virtually unlimited?

## COMPASSION WITHOUT LIMITATIONS

Though the early Christian community knew that God's compassion was without limitations, they knew equally well that God does not accept people indiscriminately regardless of how they relate to him. They had experienced the truth that no one can bypass Jesus Christ as the mediator between God and us. They had heard from Jesus: "I am the way, and the truth, and the life; no one comes to the Father, but by me" (John 14:6). But how could they reconcile God's boundless compassion and this "alone through Christ"? Here the considerations about the descent of Christ to the dead became important. If Jesus Christ had really descended into the realm of the dead after his death, through his divine nature he could not have stayed there without getting involved.

Likewise we read at the fringes of the New Testament:

For Christ also died for sins once for all, the righteous for the unrighteous, that he might bring us to God, being put to death in the flesh but made alive in the spirit; in which he went and preached to the spirits in prison, who formerly did not obey, when God's patience waited in the days of Noah . . . (1 Pet. 3:18–20).

Jesus Christ went to those who were deceased and who were waiting in the realm of death and proclaimed to them God's Word, which initially they had not accepted while still alive on earth. At another point God's compassion is so inclusive that all of humanity is included. We read: "For this is why the gospel was preached even to the dead, that though judged in the flesh like men, they might live in the spirit like God" (1 Pet. 4:6). The Christian message does not remain confined to the living but also encounters those who have already died. Even for those already destined to live forever distant from God, Jesus opens the possibility that they too are included in God's grace.

It is interesting that neither the early church fathers nor the church itself ever stated dogmatically who might have, after death, this possibility to be changed by the gospel. Some declared that all who had died before Jesus were included, and others only thought of the Old Testament patriarchs. It was clear to them, however, that Christ would include all those he was not able to meet during his lifetime. The confession that Christ descended to the realm of the dead, which has been included in the Creed, shows that Christians did not pursue some kind of salvational egotism. They were interested that as many as possible accept the powerful force of the good news. The reference to the descent into the realm of the dead is a confession of faith in the God from whose goodness we live and who seeks that no one be lost. Yet Martin Luther in his picturesque and drastic language cautioned that we should not think that at his death Jesus came with a victory flag in his hands, entering the realm of the dead, pushing open the door to the underworld, and then leading back to God the Old Testament patriarchs, among others. Nevertheless, he did assert that we must preach in such a forceful manner that people may understand our proclamation. God's compassion, which extends beyond the limits of death and is affirmed in the Creed with the term "he descended to the dead," however, should not be misconstrued as some kind of Christian imperialism.

## NO CHRISTIAN IMPERIALISM

God's compassion does not know any limits. Christ even proclaimed God's message of acceptance to those who did not have an opportunity to hear it during their earthly lives or who heard it in such a way that they could not understand it. But now we must ask whether this does not imply that God leads everybody back to God. This idea of a universal homecoming or of a universal salvation has often been taught. It presupposes that Christ died for all and concludes that, therefore, all have been saved in Jesus Christ. What is still left to do is to tell them that salvation does indeed exist. If this is no longer possible in this life, it can also happen in death.

It is true that the early Christian community decided that salvation should be proclaimed to everybody, not only to those who had been Jews or who had become Jews. The so-called gentile Christians to whom most of us owe our faith, soon spread the Christian faith among many who had been pagans. It would have been an impossible thought for the Christian community to assume that all had been saved through Jesus Christ even though many simply did not yet know it. It has always been thought important among Christians not only that one knows about the salvation brought about through Jesus Christ, but that the experience of salvation also leads to a new and different way of life. Others have frequently recognized that Christians live very differently from the way other people live. They serve a different Lord and have different guidelines for their lives.

Often one argues in favor of a universal homecoming by saying that in other religions there are many people who have ethically high standards. For instance, some years ago a well-known theologian told me: "When you look at these Japanese Shintoists and see how nice and friendly they are, one can never think seriously that they would forever live distant from God." Indeed, the idea that only those who have been Christians in this life will live eternally with God must be rejected through the confession of Christ's descent to the dead. But the Christian community has also always affirmed that we cannot work our own way back to God. An ethically high standard can be maintained through many contrasting motivations. One might be a blatant moralist simply to be better than other people; another might be afraid of being rejected by God because of his or her lax standards; another might conclude, out of genuine thankfulness for God's gracious acceptance, to lead a godly life. Our Christian life style is to be not a prerequisite for but a consequence of experiencing God's goodness.

An attitude of Christian imperialism declares that everybody will return to God because Christ has accomplished salvation for everybody. In this case, however, the individual's decision is not taken seriously. Though God wills for everyone to turn again and though we hope and pray that all will find their way back, God respects our own decisions. It is finally left to the decision of the individual what is to be made of her or his life. Yet one thing is clear. The Christian faith does not condone a salvational egotism. Very early it was taught that for those who had no possibility on earth to make a positive decision for Christ, there would be another chance after death. Exactly how this should happen was never spelled out with clarity. It was taken for granted, however, that others cannot influence the destiny of the deceased or that there is an automatic acceptance for the dead. The summons "Come to me, all who labor and are heavy laden, and I will give you rest" (Matt. 11:28) is a promise addressed to everyone regardless of when and how we lived. It attests to God's love, which is disclosed to us in Jesus Christ.

# 9 | BREAKING THE FINAL TABOO

*"On the third day he rose again."*

The apostle Paul teaches us that "if Christ has not been raised, your faith is futile and you are still in your sins" (1 Cor. 15:17). Now, many people have died for an idea or a cause, but seldom does their sacrificial death make more real that for which they died. The course of history simply bypasses their deaths, and posterity does not receive any enduring impulses through them. History hardly remembers suicidal heroes; on the contrary, it tends to remember those who perished through murder.

If we were to understand Jesus' death exclusively as self-sacrifice for the ideas that he preached, then at most his ideas would have survived. Jesus himself, however, would have perished with his death. But it is especially the person of Jesus Christ that is for the Christian faith the basis of many expectations. Of this particular person the Creed says that on the third day he "rose again." If we follow this line of thought, it would be plausible for us to interpret Jesus' resurrection in the context of our own expectations since most of us long for life eternal.

## THE YEARNING FOR LIFE ETERNAL

Human conduct is always decisively influenced by death. We might think here of the death wish that Sigmund Freud described as being in conflict with our struggle for life. Or we might consider what it means that all our striving in this life aims at negating death, as Ernest Becker has claimed. Anthropologists and ethnologists have shown us through their findings that burial rites are basic to human conduct. From time immemorial a primary human interest was not only to give last honors to the dead but also to express through burial rites a hope for those who were still alive. For instance, when the dead were buried in the crouched position, this served as a reminder that in death we return to the fetal position in which we once came into life. This expressed hope in the existence of a new life beyond our earthly one. In addition to this, the favorite burial direction is toward the East so that the buried may greet the rising sun in another life beyond death.

As soon as there were written documents, so-called books of the dead emerged, for example in Egypt and Tibet. Virtually every culture treasured concrete ideas about what awaits us beyond death and how we can steer our ultimate destiny in a positive direction. This longing for life beyond death still remains unchanged today. Even for the hard-core atheist it is a matter of fact that his or her life amounts to something that survives death. He or she lives and works for the benefit of humanity, the party, family, or some profession.

Many people to whom the resurrection makes little sense still hope that death is not the final answer. Why have reports about near-death experiences, experiences that seem to indicate a life beyond death, attracted so much attention? Even older people, who may tell us that they will be glad when everything is over, tenaciously cling to life and attempt everything possible to prolong it, perhaps because they are not sure what will come afterward. We think of death as something that ought not to be. We long for something that takes from death its grim reality and points in the direction of survival after death.

If we place Jesus' resurrection in this context of primal human desires, we are not totally mistaken. In the history of religion there are many dying gods who arose to new life so that Jesus could be counted among them. In nature too there is a cycle of growing and perishing. After the deadly cold of winter there comes a new spring, or, in other climates, after the summer drought under the merciless rays of the sun there follows a refreshing and enlivening rainy season. Paul even used the analogy that Jesus died like a kernel of wheat. But the interesting and surprising point is that according to the New Testament, Jesus did not return from the dead.

## NO RETURN FROM THE DEAD

The resurrection of Jesus is often misunderstood as a return from the dead. Perhaps the concept of resurrection can be faulted for that. When we arise after sleep, this is a return to our former life. We no longer sleep but are again awake. When we say that Jesus was raised from the dead to indicate that God the Father raised him from the dead, we still tend to remain with the image of waking from sleep and returning to conscious life.

In the New Testament we hear only seldom about a return from death to life, for instance the return of Lazarus to life or the raising of the young man at Nain. In these reports we hear that a dead person, or at least someone thought to be dead, was led back to life. Jesus' resurrection has also been explained in this way by those who claim that he only seemed to be dead and then returned to his earlier life. This idea of Jesus not really being dead is unfounded in Scripture. Equally unfounded is the explanation that Jesus was so important to his disciples that they simply could not adjust themselves to the fact that he was dead and therefore purported to have visions of his continuing life or visions of his resurrection. Such an explanation, however, deals more with the psyche of the disciples than with the historical reality of Jesus.

What is more important is that these explanations conflict with the New Testament narratives. According to the New Testament Jesus really died on Good Friday. The wound in his left side, which John mentions, conveys this quite vividly. Jesus died on the cross, and as he did so, his faintly straw-colored blood plasma separated from the red blood cells so that it was observed that from his side "came out blood and water" (John 19:34).

Very quickly Jesus' disciples had lost hope that Jesus and his movement would continue in some way after his death. This is shown dramatically in the story of the two disciples going to Emmaus. When some unknown person joined them, they told him: "But we had hoped that he [Jesus] was the one to redeem Israel" (Luke 24:21). Jesus had died; he had not returned to comfort his disciples by saying that things had not really turned out badly and promising that he could still do something for them. Even if Jesus had returned from death, he would not have provided lasting hope. Surely he would have died again later on, and we could at most find some remains of his bones. Yet the New Testament does not know about such a return to his former life.

When the New Testament tells us of the resurrection of Jesus Christ, it does not imply his returning to life. On the contrary, the resurrection means a totally new quality of life. Jesus did not return from death to this life but left death behind and entered into a totally new life. This led Paul to the triumphant claim: "Death is swallowed up in victory. O death, where is thy victory? O death, where is thy sting?" (1 Cor. 15:54–55). Death no longer had a claim on Jesus. His new form of life was no longer characterized by death and its accompanying phenomena—aging, diminishing, and perishing. The force of life that God gave through the Spirit became so powerful in Jesus Christ that he will live forever. Therefore the New Testament emphasizes that Jesus was raised through God's life-giving Spirit.

Prior to Jesus' resurrection, some of the Israelites had themselves cherished the hope in a resurrection. For instance, we read of a discussion between Jesus and the Sadducees concerning the resurrection (Matt. 22:23–25). The conservative Sadducees declined that there was hope for a resurrection, whereas the Pharisees, more influenced by the Greek spirit, affirmed that there was such a hope. The idea of a resurrection also existed in other religions, for instance in Egypt where the myth of Isis and Osiris testified to a similar hope. This being the case, however, then why should the resurrection of Jesus be so decisive that it has universal significance?

## THE UNIVERSAL SIGNIFICANCE OF CHRIST'S RESURRECTION

Hope often deceives us. Even the hope in the resurrection could finally be deceiving. It does not become credible simply because it is shared by many people. Even if one person should experience such a new state of being, there are millions of others who did not share the same experience. In this way we could at most talk about a fortunate instance. Jesus of Nazareth, so one could say, hit the jackpot and was resurrected while millions of other people who died before or after him were not so lucky. Perhaps we could show similarities between Jesus' resurrection and the destiny of Elijah or Enoch. According to the Old Testament both were brought into the immediacy of God upon their departure from this earth.

If we follow such musings, however, we thoroughly misunderstand who Jesus actually was. The New Testament witnesses affirm that Jesus was not just someone extremely fortunate, but that he was identical with God. In him God is disclosed to us. The destiny of Jesus is not just the destiny of an individual but entails God's will for all of us. As God acted in and with this human being, so also will God act in and with us. Consequently Paul confessed: "But in fact Christ has been raised from the dead, the first fruits of those who have fallen asleep. For as by a man came death, by a man has come also the resurrection of the dead" (1 Cor. 15:20–21). Jesus Christ is not just a fortunate individual who can be neglected as insignificant on the basis of statistical probability. Instead he is the exemplary case, the first one raised and thus a signal for all those who came after him.

We do not hope for a resurrection simply because we somehow have the feeling that death cannot be the last answer. We hope for resurrection because of Jesus Christ and his resurrection. Our hope is founded upon the resurrection of Jesus Christ. This means we do not believe in merely a theory or an idea of resurrection. This is also emphasized by the Creed when it reads: "On the third day he rose again." When the third day is mentioned, the resurrection of Jesus Christ is anchored in history. Three days after Good Friday he was raised to new life.

With this in mind we can now better approach the New Testament narratives that tell of the encounter with the resurrected. They show in many different ways that Jesus Christ did indeed live after his physical death and that as the resurrected one he was neither a ghost nor an apparition but a real person. He had all the possibilities of a real human being but was no longer confined by physical limitations. He went beyond that which belongs to human limitations and incompleteness. He assumed the perfection of God's being without losing his identity as a human being. This also describes our hope.

The promise of the resurrection means that upon death we will neither recede into a world soul nor enter nirvana, where we are stripped of our individuality to become one with all the other ephemeral beings. On the contrary, our individual personality will have significance before God beyond death. This has become a certainty through Christ's resurrection.

The last taboo has been broken, that is, the death barrier behind which we could not see. In the resurrection of Jesus Christ a hope has been given to us that leads us to a totally new understanding of ourselves and of the world around us. We need no longer accept this world as something ultimate and cling to it with utmost tenacity. We know that there is hope for us which makes this life livable. Our present life is already a preparation for the life to come, and therefore we can realize something of this new life in the present.

# 10 | AT THE SOURCE OF POWER

*"He ascended into heaven, and is seated at the right hand of the Father."*

When we advance to the final assertions of the second article, we encounter great conceptual difficulties. How can we conceptualize that Jesus Christ "ascended into heaven and is seated at the right hand of the Father"? The Lukan narrative of Christ's ascension is of little help in this matter since there we read even more picturesquely: "And when he had said this, as they were looking on, he was lifted up, and a cloud took him out of their sight. And while they were gazing into heaven as he went, behold, two men stood by them in white robes" (Acts 1:9–10). This explains in part our helplessness in understanding Ascension Day.

## ASCENSION—A RELIC OF THE PAST?

For most people today it is not difficult to celebrate Christmas because the gifts we exchange are an essential part of the celebration. Easter is a time when many change their wardrobes and get out their spring outfits. Pentecost, at least for church people, is the last big splash before the summer slump commences. But what shall we do with this Ascension Day, which comes in the middle of the work week on a Thursday? In Germany, for instance, where this is still a public holiday, many have turned it into Father's Day. First this was an attraction because it was thought that this was a way to challenge the church and the tradition it represents. It became a time for young men to celebrate at big parties with lots of alcohol. Many older people, however, did not care much for that. In contrast to Mother's

Day which always centers on mother, Father's Day in Germany thus has hardly anything to do with actual fathers. In the United States, where Ascension Day does not enjoy government recognition, the churches are not better off. Some still hold an Ascension Day service in the evening but with little success since most people do not attend. Even celebrating Ascension Day the following Sunday does not make much difference. It is just another Sunday.

We might ask why we should still maintain such a festival in the twentieth century. For most of us this day is certainly not as unknown as it was to the little boy who, when told by his mother that the next day was Ascension Day, responded: "Oh, that's nice, Mother. May I go there too?" We might be tempted to dispense with Ascension Day saying that today reasonable people can hardly believe that Jesus was lifted from earth just like a rocket takes off and then goes toward the sky. We no longer share the world view of a three-story universe with heaven above, earth in the middle, and the nether regions below, a concept that is hidden behind the image of ascension. Above us is not heaven but the sky, and below us is the interior of the earth.

Before we reject too quickly Christ's ascension as no longer fitting for our time, however, we should listen to Martin Luther. He was not yet a child of our time and still lived in a pre-Copernican universe. The earth was thought of as a flat disk above which the firmament stretched out like a cheese cover and which continuously changed, as indicated by the daily path of the sun. Ulrich Zwingli, the reformer of Zürich, attempted to localize Jesus at the right hand of God, clinging literally to the Bible. Therefore, he held the simultaneous presence of Christ in the Lord's Supper to be impossible. But Martin Luther responded to him that we should not think of Jesus Christ as sitting on a stool at the right hand of God somewhere "up there." If this were the case, Luther objected, Christ could not sit still for one moment because the firmament continuously moves and Christ would always be in danger of falling off his chair. At another time Luther objected that sitting at the right hand of God should not be conceptualized as if Christ were sitting somewhere up there "like a stork in its nest."

Luther was convinced that the biblical assertions about Christ ascending into heaven and sitting at the right hand of God were not intended to describe some heavenly geography. Nevertheless, these pictures were to convey an important message. The mention of Christ's ascending into heaven and sitting at the right hand of God the Father Almighty does not imply a geographical location so that we know where we can find Christ. If that were so, we could assume that he disappeared from this earth into some kind of better beyond without still remaining in contact with us. In contrast to such ideas, Paul stated that Christ's ascension was the consequence of his obedience. Paul wrote: "Therefore God has highly exalted him and bestowed on him the name which is above every name, that at the name of Jesus every knee should bend, in heaven and on earth and under the earth, and every tongue confess that Jesus Christ is Lord, to the glory of God the Father" (Phil. 2:9–11).

The exaltation of Jesus Christ has nothing to do with a geographic locale but with his enthronement into the fullness of God's power. Underlying this is the Old Testament promise that the psalmist expressed in Psalm 110: "The LORD says to my lord: 'Sit at my right hand, till I make your enemies your footstool'" (Ps. 110:1). This word of God was initially addressed to the king of Jerusalem. The God who had chosen Israel promises to the king that he will one day rule the entire world. God alone will put the king's enemies at his feet. Sitting to the right hand of God emphasizes the king's special power and honor. In the ancient Near East the place to the right hand of an emperor was conferred upon the person who was next in power and who could exercise it in the emperor's name. When God says to the king that he is to sit at God's right hand, this means that the king is given the power to rule the world in God's name.

The early church understood this passage as a messianic promise and applied it to Jesus Christ. This was certainly justified, since in the Jewish faith this psalm pointed to the coming Messiah. When Jesus Christ was recognized as the Messiah on the basis of his sacrificial death and his resurrection, he was also understood as the fulfiller of this messianic promise. Jesus Christ was described as being exalted to the right hand of God. At God's side he rules the world in God's name. The confession of the ascended Christ, who sits at the right hand of God, follows naturally once we realize his significance as the crucified and resurrected one. Jesus Christ did not take off from this earth in order to remain aloof from our affairs somewhere in the universe. On the contrary, he is present where the decisions are made, and this means he is with God. He is not a detached spectator but participates in these decisions in God's name. Therefore the ascension is the sign of Christ's power.

## THE RISE TO POWER

Some theologians claim, perhaps with some justification, that initially there was no distinction between the resurrection and the ascension of Jesus Christ. Jesus did not haunt the earth like a ghost or a spirit until he finally assumed his place at the right hand of God. Rather, through his resurrection he was raised immediately to the right hand of God. From there he showed himself to his disciples as the one who had broken through the barrier of death and who enabled a new life for them and all the faithful.

When the church celebrated the ascension later as a separate festival, it did this to emphasize that Jesus Christ is really the Lord. He did not leave this earth behind but remains connected with it in an integral way, since as God's representative he governs its destiny. When the disciples did not want to turn their eyes from Jesus as he physically left them, they were immediately reprimanded: "Men of Galilee, why do you stand looking into heaven? This Jesus, who was taken up from you into heaven, will come in the same way as you saw him go into heaven" (Acts 1:11). Jesus Christ's departure is no reason for mourning since he did not leave his people alone. Martin Luther emphasized many times that through his exaltation Jesus Christ now is present to all of us wherever we are, and he is especially so when we celebrate his Meal. Jesus Christ is no absentee landlord. He is present in and with his church. This means that he is also present with each of us and we can call upon him and talk with him.

The early church, however, went one step further in its reflections. In calling Jesus Christ the Lord it wanted to show that he is the Lord of the whole world. Thus Jesus Christ was also called the Word (Greek: *logos*) who had become flesh (John 1:14). In the Greek philosophy of that time, the term *logos* had still another important meaning. It was understood as the reason and order that permeate the whole world. Describing Christ as the *logos* leads us to another aspect of his ascension and exaltation, the affirmation that the right hand of God is all-present.

## THE SIGN OF CHRIST'S OMNIPRESENCE

The early Christian church realized that Christ is not confined to the church. If Jesus Christ is ruling the world as God's representative, we should feel his presence even beyond the church. The first Christian theologians noted that, to their surprise, the so-called pagans had many insights which were similar to the insights obtainable through Christian faith. Some Christians claimed that the pagans had gained this knowledge from the Old Testament. But much more plausible was the assumption that the incarnate *logos* was also present throughout the world in a seminal way. Thus one could explain how outside the Christian faith, for instance in other religions, there were fitting and knowledgeable insights. Jesus Christ was present there in his omnipresence, not however in his specific personal presence in which the Christian community still encounters him today. Only the Christian faith allows for an adoration of Christ, whereas in other religions he is, at most, implicitly venerated.

The confession of Christ's ascension to the right hand of God cannot be ignored by us, though the images involved may cause misunderstanding. If we expect anything significant to come from Christ today, this confession is not optional.

For Christians Jesus Christ is not an ideal of the past so that we merely are inspired as we are by other great people. Jesus Christ is not someone who lives distant from this earth, somewhere beyond the sky, in a better hereafter. For the Christians and for the whole world, Jesus Christ is the Lord. He is at the center of power and determines the ultimate destiny of this world. This does not mean, however, that we have no room to decide against him. Like God, Jesus Christ is no tyrant whom we must blindly obey as puppets. The suffering we cause through our anti-Christian and unreasonable behavior shows only too well that we always succeed in ignoring Christ's rule. But the messianic promise tells us that in Jesus Christ the world will find its completion and its destiny. Before him all knees will one day have to bend, and all of us will one day have to recognize him as our Lord.

Until then we have only the promise that is connected with his ascension and his sitting at the right hand of God. It tells us that we are not confronted in this life with a neutral cosmos or an unyielding destiny but with a world government which has assumed personal features in Jesus Christ. The one who ultimately decides about this world and about our destiny is the same one who spoke of himself this way in a parable: "I came that they may have life, and have it abundantly. . . . I am the good Shepherd" (John 10:10–11).

# 11 | FROM JUDGE OF THE WORLD TO HOPE OF THE WORLD

*"He will come again to judge the living and the dead."*

The last phrase in the second article of the Creed proclaims of Jesus: "He will come again to judge the living and the dead." Jesus Christ will return from his position of power at the right hand of God to judge the living and the dead. This confession of Jesus as the judge of the world is well known to those of us who have been in Europe and seen the portals of medieval churches. Many of them portray the scene of the last judgment. Jesus Christ sits on his throne and gathers on the right those who will be accepted, while on the left are those who will be punished with eternal suffering. The faces of the people he has already judged reflect their eternal destiny. Of course, such stone-hewn scenes are only images or parables reminding us that this world will come to an end and that all of us will then be accountable for what we have done and left undone in this life. The Christian faith shares the expectation of such an end of our lives and the world with almost all religions.

## THE EXPECTATION OF THE END

In the teachings of all religions there seems to be the desire to protect the faithful so that the end of their lives and the end of the world are not experienced as horrifying but rather as desirable. Especially today, as major world religions seem to be reawakening, preparation for the day of reckoning is again being taken quite seriously. In many Muslim countries one attempts to live rigorously according to the laws of the Koran because in this way one hopes that Allah will be gracious at death. One does not even shy away from political-ideological suicide missions because Mohammed promised that everybody who dies for the cause of Allah will be immediately received into a better beyond. In other religions there are other ways to escape the coming wrath of judgment, such as fasting, doing good works, or ceaselessly chanting prayers.

For a long time many threatening ideas about the end of the world were prevalent in Christendom. For instance, Martin Luther grew up being confronted with a threatening, merciless God who demanded accountability and who would one day send his son to judge the world. The proverbial "book of life" in which all our actions are recorded was a life-determining and life-threatening reality for Luther. It was certainly not due to his love for monastic life that Luther abandoned his studies of jurisprudence and joined a monastery. Rather, his fear of Christ as the judge of the world drove him to that decision. Similar fears led many others to do the same thing. We are also reminded here of the "pillar saints" in the early church, who in self-inflicted discipline chose to live their lives on high pillars, or of the famous theologian Origen who castrated himself in his attempt to lead a God-pleasing life. Today many of us may only smile at such religious rigorism or fanaticism. In our time the Christian faith is not to be taken that seriously.

Fear still haunts us today, however. Perhaps it is not the fear of God's ushering in the end of the world, but we fear nonetheless the possibility of an end caused by our obsession to protect ourselves against potential enemies with ever more dangerous weapons. In quiet moments we often feel ourselves haunted by fear and feel uneasy as we begin to think about the future. This may be one of the reasons why we turn on the radio day in and day out and why our television sets often run whether we are watching them or not. We cannot stand the silence of being alone. We want to drown out our feelings of uncertainty regarding what might come and hide our doubts as to whether the end will really be bright.

Our fear has changed from a religious fear to a worldly fear. But our fear about the future has nevertheless remained in both a penultimate and an ultimate sense. We may try to persuade ourselves that we have to live with the bomb, but we still want to know whether the end will come out all right. When we attempt to live for the moment so that nothing escapes us, we soon realize that fulfillment is not found in running with the crowd. At the most we feel worn out and have to live with a heavy head on the day after a fling. Even if we succeed in forgetting the world and its problems for a few hours, we cannot escape our own transitoriness. No matter what we try, after a few hours we are always thrown back into the world. If there is fulfillment of life, then it must be beyond this life. As we sing in a Christmas song, "Your coming in the darkest night/Makes us children of the light." This "transformation from beyond" is vitally important for the Christian faith. Christian theologians emphasize this when they almost unanimously characterize Jesus' message as an eschatological (end-time) message.

Jesus and his message have something to do with the end of the world. This becomes readily evident when we think of the prayer that Jesus taught his disciples, which we usually pray in church services. In the Lord's Prayer we say: "Thy Kingdom come, thy will be done, on earth as it is in heaven." This prayer is an expression of the hope and desire that the divine will one day permeate the whole world. All the anti-godly and destructive powers under which we now suffer will no longer have a reason for existence. In order to inaugurate the will of God, however, power is necessary. Therefore we confess Christ as the returning Lord, the judge whose judgment will have eternal consequences. Then we must ask how Jesus can be our judge when he has also called himself the good shepherd.

## CAN A SAVIOR BE A JUDGE?

The question as to how the two images of Jesus as the judge and the savior of the world can be reconciled, can be answered quite easily when we understand that behind our confession of Christ returning from heaven to judge the living and the dead is a vision from the book of the prophet Daniel. There we read:

> I saw in the night visions, and behold, with the clouds of heaven there came one like the son of man, and he came to the Ancient of Days and was presented before him. And to him was given dominion and glory and kingdom, that all peoples, nations, and languages should serve him; his dominion is an everlasting dominion, which shall not pass

away, and his kingdom one that shall not be destroyed (Dan. 7:13-14).

This Son of man is also mentioned in the Apocalypse of Enoch, where his main task consists of being the judge at the end time. The tradition of the Son of man who comes on the clouds of heaven is again picked up by Jesus.

Several times Jesus talked about the Son of man, but usually in the third person. At the trial before the Sanhedrin, for instance, we read that the high priest addressed Jesus with this decisive question: "'Are you the Christ, the Son of the Blessed?' And Jesus said: 'I am; and you will see the Son of man sitting at the right hand of Power, and coming with the clouds of heaven'" (Mark 14:61-62). This confession of Jesus regarding himself and the coming Son of man quickly terminated the trial. As a pious Jew who had heard blasphemy, the high priest tore his garment. For those who had not understood the meaning of Jesus' response, the high priest asserted that blasphemy had taken place. Jesus had dared to identify himself with this end-time figure, the Son of man. According to Jewish understanding, Jesus had committed blasphemy because in this way he had also equated himself with God. The response of the high priest and the Sanhedrin was certainly drastic but also consistent: Jesus is guilty and he must die.

The early church affirmed Jesus' own confession. It realized, however, that the Son of man could not be a separate figure next to Jesus even though he himself had mostly talked about the Son of man in the third person during his life on earth. Rather, the Son of man must be identical with Jesus Christ. The evidence for this conclusion was found in the resurrection of Christ.

In the early Christian community there developed no fear complexes about equating Jesus with the returning judge of the world. Quite the opposite. Many Christians hoped intensively for the return of Christ, which they expected in the near future. This even prompted some Christians in Jerusalem to abandon their personal property and any long-range planning for the future as they began to share everything in common. The apostle Paul, who also counted on an early return of Christ, was concerned about such oblivion to the world and felt obligated to ask for donations for the brothers and sisters in Jerusalem who were threatened with starvation. The return of Christ should not be misunderstood as a heavenly utopia that leads us to neglect the necessities of this life. Soon it was also remembered, however, that Jesus himself had said that nobody knows of the time or the hour of the end.

We see from the petitions in the Lord's Prayer that the Christian faith still clings to the conviction that Christ will one day return. Exactly when this will happen remains God's own secret. Today some may think that this end-time component of the Christian faith can be eliminated without any cause for concern. It has been suggested that it is sufficient to understand Christ as the savior of the world. Why should one still think of him as the judge of the world? With this kind of reasoning, however, we also render meaningless the significance of Christ as the savior of the world.

Let us illustrate this by considering the profession of a medical doctor. According to our expectations a doctor should heal the patient. Often this is done by prescribing some medicine. Yet if the disease is of a more severe nature, a doctor may have to send the patient to the hospital for an operation. Healing means in this case to eliminate that which is bad for the patient, such as an ulcer, a tumor, or a virus. A doctor without the authority to do all that is necessary to heal the patient would be a quack. In a similar way Jesus Christ would only be a moralistic preacher if he were a savior who had no authority for judgment. Our lives and the world itself would continue indefinitely with its never ending mixture of good and bad. Our hopes and desires, however, long for a point when this mixture will finally be separated so that all evil and destructive forces will be eliminated. This is shown at the conclusion of the Lord's Prayer where we pray: "For thine is the kingdom, and the power, and the glory, forever and ever. Amen."

## THE MANIFESTATION OF THE KINGDOM

Inseparably connected with the Christian faith is the conviction that the kingdom of God, which started with Christ's coming, will one day be made manifest. There will be a time when all incompleteness and fragmentariness will be taken up into the completion of God. When we look carefully at our lives, however, we notice so many incomplete and fragmentary items that we ask ourselves whether we can survive such a general cleansing of the world. This question had already been asked by pious people of both the Old and the New Testament. It seems that only someone who does not really care about God can live with the illusion that God is a "good guy" who at the end will forgive because that is God's job. If we share this idea about God, we have not yet realized how deeply our lives differ from the way God intends them to be. Again, however, the question emerges whether this image of God as our judge should not cause us to fear it.

At this point it is important for us to recall the words of Paul when he said: "If any one is in Christ, he is a new creation; the old has passed away, behold, the new has come" (2 Cor. 5:17). Our lives may be a total mess but when we cling to Christ and his liberating word, judgment has already been passed. Christ will not forget the inadequacy of our lives, but he will make up for them. It was the hope of the early Christian community and it remains our hope today that Christ sacrificed himself for all who want to be on his side. Thus the immense chasm between God and humanity has been bridged.

Here lies the difference between salvation portrayed by most world religions and the understanding of Christ as judge in the Christian faith. While in other religions the attempt is made to bridge the chasm between human beings and the divine through various religious exercises, in the Christian faith we realize that the rift cannot be healed from our side. Only God can open to us the way to divine communion. It is the Christian conviction that this has happened through the life, death, and resurrection of Jesus Christ. Therefore, Jesus is not a threatening judge but, instead, the hope of the world. He has given his life for us so that we can have eternal life. As Luther once put it, a Christian is a free person who obeys God alone.

The certainty that in Christ the chasm between God and us has been bridged allows us to turn to the world and its needs. There is no need for us to separate ourselves from the world and seek our own ways toward salvation. Rather, we are free to act responsibly in this world wherever God has placed us. The manifestation of God's kingdom is for us not only an event that will occur one day at the end of this world but something to which we can already bear witness now. Our anticipation of the kingdom does not lead us to an earthly utopia or the idea that we ourselves can build the kingdom of God on earth. Yet it does call us to witness to God and God's kingdom in all our actions, knowing that God rejects everything which is contrary to God. Thus we endeavor to become Christlike to our fellow human beings and witness to them that through Christ the darkness of this world will one day give way to new light.

# 12 | THE POWER OF LIFE

*"I believe in the Holy Spirit . . ."*

We now turn to the third article of the Apostles' Creed, which focuses on the work of the Holy Spirit. Immediately we notice that there is only one short reference to the Holy Spirit in the introductory passage. Then we hear about the church, the forgiveness of sins, the resurrection of the dead, and life eternal. Martin Luther, however, in his explanation of the third article, recognized that all these items that we just mentioned are the result of the Holy Spirit's working. They are like stepping stones that God has placed before us so that we may come back to God. Without God's help we may try as hard as we can, but we will always fall back to this earth and its limitations.

The work of the Holy Spirit is greater, however, than even these vital concerns. When we confine the effects of the Holy Spirit to those of making us acceptable to God and bringing us in tune with the origin of our life, we restrict the Holy Spirit to a solely inner Christian phenomenon. Though it may look as though Christians have a lease on the Holy Spirit, we do not know much about the Spirit. In the Apostles' Creed the Spirit is only mentioned on the fringe, almost as one additional item among others. This expresses very eloquently that the Holy Spirit has received only secondary consideration by the Christian church.

## THE HOLY SPIRIT AS AN AFTERTHOUGHT

When asked what the Holy Spirit is or how the Spirit affects us, most of us begin to stutter. With Jesus Christ we can connect the human figure of Jesus of Nazareth. With God our task is more difficult because the great acts of God such as the exodus from Egypt and the occupation of the promised land are relatively remote from our experience. This may also be one of the reasons why the name of God is so often used in vain. With the Holy Spirit, however, it is almost impossible to connect a concrete experience. Occasionally we may refer to something as "dispirited" or talk about "the spirit of the times." Or we may talk about spirits, meaning alcoholic beverages. How such phrases can be connected to the Holy Spirit remains unclear. Even when we consider the Holy Spirit as a spirit or ghost, we are not closer to a solution. Spirits are usually thought of as ghosts that go a-haunting and are considered an absurdity in our enlightened age.

Of course most of us know that the Holy Spirit is somehow connected with the birth of the church and the pouring out of the Spirit at Pentecost. But what actually happened then is difficult for most of us to comprehend. We also hear occasionally about gifts of the Spirit. But those who most fervently advocate them usually just mention one gift, that of speaking in tongues. What this phenomenon entails is rarely experienced outside Pentecostal circles, and consequently access is closed for many of us.

In our sense of loss about the Holy Spirit we are in good company because even the early church had a difficult time determining the function of the Holy Spirit. From the Old Testament it was evident that the Holy Spirit is the Spirit of God. But we also know that Jesus Christ is the Son of God whom God sent into the world through his Spirit. Therefore, the angel said to Mary in announcing the birth of Jesus: "The Holy Spirit will come upon you, and the power of the Most High will overshadow you; therefore the child to be born will be called holy, the Son of God" (Luke 1:35). How then are Father, Son, and Holy Spirit related to each other? Are they of equal value, subordinated to each other, or simply different concepts for one and the same agent?

The church soon realized that there is an intimate relationship between Jesus, the Son of God, and the Holy Spirit as the power of God. In some ways the Son and the Spirit of God can be seen as a unity. Yet one should not treat them indiscriminately because, in contrast to the Spirit, the Son has a concrete historical reference point in the human being Jesus of Nazareth. Since such a historical anchor is missing for the Spirit, it is, on the one hand, less historically concrete and, on the other hand, more comprehensive in its activity. This concept showed itself especially clearly at the Council of Constantinople (A.D. 381), where the Nicene Creed was enlarged to its present form in order to emphasize the function of the Spirit. There it was expressly stated that Jesus Christ had become human through the Holy Spirit from the virgin Mary. This means that the incarnation of Jesus can only be understood as an effect of the Holy Spirit. We also read in the new version of the Creed that the Holy Spirit is "the Lord, the giver of life," that he "proceeds from the Father and the Son," that "with the Father and the Son he is worshiped and glorified" and that "he has spoken through the prophets."

Most of these references can be traced to biblical precedents. Like Jesus Christ, the Holy Spirit is called the Lord. While Jesus Christ gives new life, the Spirit is understood as the one who gives life in general. With this reference the life-creating power of the Spirit is introduced, which is especially important in the Old Testament. The statement that the Spirit has spoken through the prophets again refers us to the Old Testament. The prophets were men and women gifted by the Spirit, through whom God spoke when giving promises to the people of Israel or when scolding them because of their trespasses. Though mention is also made of the adoration of the Spirit together with the Father and the Son, Constantinople did not want to identify the Spirit with the Father and the Son. It was not conceded that the Holy Spirit was of one being with the Father. High honor is to be attributed to the Spirit, and it is even worshiped, but it is not God. A difference remains between God's Spirit and God. In this way the Spirit is God's medium for permeating the world.

## THE MEDIUM FOR PERMEATING THE WORLD

While we often talk about the autonomy of life and the innate laws of nature, the earthy Israelites were convinced that nothing originates out of nothing. The best cattle-breeding techniques do not amount to anything if there is no forage, and the best agricultural methods are without success if there is no rain. The Israelites knew that there was a natural cause and effect system. Of course, they did not know it as thoroughly as we know it today through intensive research. But they did know that without material causes there were no material effects. It was beyond their conception, however, that all there is to nature is that which is material. For instance, in the Book of Job the rhetorical question is posed: "Who gave him charge over the earth and who laid on him the whole world? If he should take back his spirit to himself, and gather to himself his breath, all flesh would perish together, and man would return to dust" (Job 34:13–15). Without God nothing can survive in this world. It is God's Spirit who creates life and if God turns the Spirit from us, we return to lifeless matter.

The Spirit of God affects the difference not only between life and death but also between knowing and not knowing. Again we read in the Book of Job: "But it is the spirit in a man, the breath of the Almighty, that makes him understand" (Job 32:8). Neither age nor education mediate wisdom. We may be extremely proud of our achievements in science and technology, but without the Spirit of God who entrusted to us this earth and to whom we owe our life, we would still be in the dark. Without the Spirit this world is not only without comfort but also without love.

Perhaps no one has experienced more strongly our modern loss of orientation and direction than Friedrich Nietzsche, as he exclaimed in *The Gay Science:*

> Where do we move? Backwards, sidewards, forwards, in all direc-
> tions? Is there still an above and below? Do we not wander as through
> infinite nothingness? Does not empty space breathe on us? Has it not
> become colder? Is it not continuously night and more night?

We know so much but have not become wiser; we know so much about humankind but are ever more helpless when confronted with our fellow human beings; we have largely succeeded in controlling nature and its laws, but we do not understand them. If we separate ourselves from the one who holds everything together, we lose our sense for the whole. By excluding the question of meaning, our actions become meaningless. We cannot forfeit the Spirit of God without losing our own spirit. If we separate our secular pursuits from God's wisdom, we are forced to replace God's wisdom with a secular ideology.

We cannot ignore God's means for permeating the world without losing the reality of God's presence. For instance, the Egyptian pharaoh was looking for an administrator filled by the Spirit of God so that he could master the problems connected with a threatening famine (Gen. 41:38). Perhaps the pharaoh thought that a person who is in tune with God's Spirit could not be a hardhearted technocrat but would have a sense of the needs of the people. When Joseph was chosen and given the authority to procure food for the Egyptians, he did not abuse his position or use it for his own advantage. He did his best to soften the impact of the famine in Egypt and the neighboring lands. He also did not seek revenge on his brothers for the evil they had done him but asked the Spirit of God for right conduct. Since the Spirit of God is intimately connected with God, he was thus the sign of God's presence.

## THE SIGN OF GOD'S PRESENCE

We can see from passages such as Psalm 51:10-12 that the Holy Spirit is understood as the sign of God's presence. There the psalmist says: "Create in me a clean heart, O God, and put a new and right spirit within me. Cast me not away from thy presence, and take not thy holy Spirit from me. Restore to me the joy of thy salvation, and uphold me with a willing spirit." A pure heart corresponds here with a new and steady spirit. As long as the Holy Spirit is with us, we can survive. Equipped with God's willing Spirit, we gain joy in our life. Our spirit must be continuously nourished by God's Spirit so that we know the difference between good and evil, true and false, confidence and dejection.

God's Spirit is the power of life that connects us with the source of life. Therefore, it was one of the great expectations of Israel that at the end time God would pour out the Spirit upon humanity in such fullness that this overwhelming power of life would make death impossible. At the same time the fullness of God's Spirit would also lead to right conduct. This promise for the end time is expressed in Ezekiel: "A new heart I will give you, and a new spirit I will put within you; and I will take out of your flesh the heart of stone and give you a heart of flesh. And I will put my spirit within you, and cause you to walk in my statutes and be careful to observe my ordinances" (Ezek. 36:26-27). Nevertheless the following vision in Ezekiel, in which God raises to new life the bones of the deceased through the mediation of the Spirit, remains only a vision. Israel continues to turn away from God and to ignore the Spirit. The people die as they have always done and have no part through God's Spirit in the power of life.

With Jesus and his coming the picture changes. Jesus was sent into this world through God's Spirit. When the unspirited conduct of his fellow Jews brought Jesus' death, he was raised to new life through God's Spirit. In the resurrection of Jesus Christ the Spirit of God overcame the death barrier for the first time. Statistically, we would argue that Jesus' resurrection was such a singular case that we are not able to derive hope from it. If we condone such thoughts, however, we forget that Jesus went to death representing us. This means that he represents us also in his resurrection. For his sake we are allowed to experience a resurrection like his to a new and unperishable form of life. This, however, would only refer to some future event if the miracle of Pentecost had not occurred.

The pouring out of the Holy Spirit, that is, participation in the fullness of God's Spirit, was something the pious people of the Old Testament desired for themselves at the end of time. Through the miracle of Pentecost, however, this event has already taken place in an anticipatory way, even though in a universal and all-encompassing way it will still occur at the end of history. God has poured out the Spirit over Christians. Therefore we may hope that the presence of God, which is expressed by this pouring out of the Spirit, will have significance beyond death.

Through the Spirit working in and with us, God is no longer far away from us. God is not enthroned, benign and distant, somewhere above the stars. Through God's Spirit God has come close to us so that we can make our decisions and conduct our life in the Spirit. Of course, Christians still live in this world and are subject to its temptations. Yet they know, as Paul said, that Jesus Christ as the last Adam has become a life-giving Spirit (1 Cor. 15:45). If we side with Jesus Christ and are baptized in his name, we can participate in the life-giving power of the Spirit. We need no longer be afraid of the world and can exclaim with Paul: "Death is swallowed up in victory. O death, where is thy victory? O death, where is thy sting?" (1 Cor. 15:54–55). God's Spirit gives us a new orientation that goes beyond the imminent limitations of this world. Thus the dream of Archimedes, the famous Greek scientist of antiquity, has been realized: there is indeed a fixed point outside the world from which we can give the world a new turn. The world in its present condition will be changed from its incompletion and sinfulness; the Spirit of God will permeate it and direct it toward Christ. God's Spirit is the new power of life, which overcomes all of this world's incompleteness.

Quite tellingly, the pouring out of the Spirit is connected with the miracle of language. In contrast to the egotistic divisions of humanity at Babel, where the attempt was made to dethrone God by erecting a tall tower, here, at Pentecost, a universal communion with God was discovered anew. Participating in the Spirit, we recognize God as our Father and the people around us as brothers and sisters. In our belief in the Holy Spirit we come to trust this all-permeating power of life. The Holy Spirit is not an anonymous and obscure entity but rather the source from which we gain our life and toward which we can orient it. Once we discover this source anew and understand it rightly, our life will not remain without comfort and strength. We will discover happiness and will begin to radiate the life-giving Spirit that we have received. We should praise and rejoice in the God who gives us this Spirit.

# 13 | THE CHURCH— LEGACY AND LIABILITY

*". . . the holy catholic church, the*
*communion of saints . . . "*

How can we claim to believe in a holy catholic church and the communion of saints without at once expressing many doubts? Very few experience the church as holy, and even when we use the word "Christian" to describe the church we may add a question mark. It appears all too obvious that the church does not live up to its professed attributes. Protestants, moreover, have an especially difficult time with the term "communion of saints" because they shy away from any veneration of the saints.

Many people simply do not know what to do with the church. Barely 60 percent of the U.S. population belongs to a church. Often the church is equated with a pastor or with a certain structure. Protesting the prevalent secularized attitude and the anonymity of the major denominations, many sects have emerged in the course of history which, in their fervent zeal, have attempted to return to the early Christians' seriousness about belonging to the church. After a few generations, however, these sects become hardly distinguishable from the major churches from which they separated. They tend to lose much of their warmth and become comfortably established.

When we, in the third article, confess our faith in the holy catholic church and the communion of saints, then, in contrast to faith in the Holy Spirit, we are expected not to believe "in" a holy catholic church but to commit ourselves to it. The church is not in itself an object of faith. Instead, we are expected to commit ourselves to it. The wording of the statement also does not imply that we confess our allegiance to a particular ecclesiastical community, for instance to the Roman Catholic church or the Evangelical Lutheran church in America, but to the *one church* as it was brought into life through the pouring out of the Holy Spirit.

The communion of saints thus does not exist separately from this holy catholic church but is identical with it. With this notion we have arrived at an understanding of the church that Martin Luther described when he said: "Thank God, a seven-year-old child knows what the church is, namely, holy believers and sheep who hear the voice of their shepherd." The church we confess in the third article is not limited to a peculiar denomination but transcends all the denominational boundaries that we have drawn to define ourselves over against other Christians. In this way the Nicene Creed, like the Apostles' Creed, confesses one holy, common (or catholic), and apostolic church.

We never experience this holy catholic church, however, in its pure form but only in its historical concretion of a certain denomination. Through its historical context the church not only becomes concrete but also becomes tarnished through historical errors and mistakes. The church that we confess is, so to speak, the ideal core which is hidden within the hard and sometimes abrasive shell of historical concretion. We should not identify this core, the communion of saints, with the historical realization of any particular denomination. If we were to do so, we would quickly be forced to discard the church as insufficient. Instead, we must pursue the opposite course and constantly compare the historical embodiment of the church with its core. Quite often we come to suffer from the church and the insufficient ways in which it manifests the community of saints. But only by comparing it with its essence and goal can the church be continuously reformed and redirected. Therefore the Augsburg Confession defines the church according to its goal: "It is also taught among us that one holy Christian church will be and remain forever. This is the assembly of all believers among whom the gospel is preached in its purity and the holy sacraments are administered according to the Gospel."

The church can come to symbolize many different things, and it can also lose itself in many peripheral pursuits. Yet according to its essence it should focus on three aims: remembering the past, helping to supply an orientation in the present, and pointing to a new and undeserved future.

## REMEMBERING THE PAST

Some people consider the church as a relic of the past. This is justified insofar as the church cannot be thought of without recalling the past that the church preserves in still vivid memory. When we think of the organ works of Johann Sebastian Bach or the frescos of Michelangelo in the Sistine Chapel in Rome or the famous Isenheim altar of Matthias Grünewald, we quickly notice that these cultural achievements are unthinkable without the church. If we were to eliminate from culture the religious component, we would have to destroy in an unprecedented way a host of pictures and monuments from the past. In our Western world the churches are in a unique way preservers of culture. This is also the case with other religions in other cultural contexts. If the church, however, only serves to remind us of the past in this way, it could easily be likened to a museum. Thus it is important to recognize that the church also makes a more existential connection with the past.

When the Augsburg Confession describes the church as the assembly of all believers among whom the gospel is preached in its purity and the sacraments are administered according to the Gospel, then three reference points emerge: the communion of believers, the gospel, and the sacraments—each of which is deeply anchored in the past.

When we study history we notice how much we owe to the past. How much insight, how much faith, and how much dedication we encounter on every page of the history of the church! When in the first centuries the church was mercilessly persecuted, the blood of the martyrs came to be called the seed of the church. Analogously we can say that the Christians of the past are our fathers and mothers in faith from whom we learn what it means to be a Christian. We may think here of Augustine and his *Confessions,* of Count Nicholas of Zinzendorf and the Brethren, or of Dietrich Bonhoeffer and his *Letters and Papers from Prison.* These ancestors in faith have influenced innumerable people and given them hope and new strength. We could extend our list of names at will and would soon realize more and more that the communion of saints, or assembly of believers, is not confined to the present. We are not the first Christians but are closely connected with the past through the impulses that our forebears in faith gave us and continue to give us. The communion of saints is a communion of Christians of all times, people, and countries who allow themselves to be sanctified and strengthened through the Holy Spirit. The reference to the past must still be recognized in another way.

The two focal points around which the Christian community gathers, preaching of the gospel and administration of the sacraments, are anchored in history. Through the proclamation of the gospel the Christian community remembers the great acts of God, which culminated in the sending of God's Son. The sacraments, of which the Lord's Supper and Baptism are of prime importance, actualize what Jesus Christ has done for us. We are taken into his death and celebrate his resurrection in these sacraments not just by remembering a noble person of the past but by their effectiveness as signs that point to a new creation which is to a certain degree already present. The presence of Jesus Christ in them, through the power of the Spirit, becomes understandable as we recall who Jesus was and is. Since the Christian faith is no timeless philosophy of life but a conviction based on God's acts in history, we may go beyond the mere interpretations of life provided by philosophers. The promise contained in gospel and sacrament shows that we may also expect a change of life. The transformation of this present world, as demanded by Karl Marx, is an accomplished matter of fact for Christians. Confronted with the uncertainty of the present, the church also serves as a point of orientation.

## ORIENTATION IN THE PRESENT

The church has often deviated from its mandate to provide an orientation for the life of people. The lengthy struggle over investiture by the emperor in the High Middle Ages and the inquisition at the beginning of the Reformation show how much the church wanted to change the course of history by changing the affairs of the world. We too desire quite often that the church be involved in this or that matter in our country. Yet if the church really wants to follow Jesus Christ, then imposing itself on others and wielding worldly power is unfitting. The church must seek to exchange the bishops' staff for a walking stick. Confronted with magnificently impressive medieval bishops' residences, it must realize that the Son of man had nowhere to lay his head. To be a Christian church means to be a servant church.

Recent research has shown that the Lord's Supper is not only connected with the last supper that Jesus celebrated with his disciples but also with the meals that he shared with sinners and the outcasts of society. For us, however, the church and its sacraments have largely become phenomena of suburbia. Of course, the church has vastly expanded its concern for others, but in so doing has it become a church that really makes welcome in its midst those who are outcast and despised in society?

Jesus said to his disciples that when the Son of man returns in glory he will say to those at his right hand: "I was hungry and you gave me food, I was thirsty and you gave me drink, I was a stranger and you welcomed me, I was naked and you clothed me, I was sick and you visited me, I was in prison and you came to me" (Matt. 25:35–36). Will it also be said of us that we were looking out for the poor and the powerless? In a world in which the loudest voices and the strongest elbows usually win, the church must continuously show in word and deed that in the end the winners are not those who never yield but rather those who give themselves for others. In a cold and ruthless world the church should resemble the warming light of God's love. Though the church cannot change the world by its own power, it should bear witness to a change of values that it practices in its own midst.

The church will inevitably contain worldly features. If there is no difference, however, between world and church, then the salt has become bland (Matt. 5:13) and the church is no longer a leaven (Matt. 13:33) that seeks to quicken those who try to rest quietly distant from God. At the same time, the church is not a community of idealists who out of some masochistic pleasure derived from a different ideology want to swim against the stream. The power and encouragement to lead a life of humility and devotion come only from the fact that the church is the pointer to a new and undeserved future.

## POINTER TO A NEW FUTURE

According to Matthew, Jesus promised Peter: "You are Peter, and on this rock I will build my church, and the powers of death shall not prevail against it" (Matt. 16:18). According to a widespread interpretation of this passage, Jesus here founded the Petrine office, which has its continuation in the present-day papacy. The claim has also been made that in this passage Jesus founded the church. The most important aspect of this promise, however, is neither the Petrine office nor the establishment of the church but the affirmation that the powers of darkness will not gain the victory over either the church or that which it represents. One could interpret the relationship between these powers of darkness and the church as God's institution in such a way that they are seen to be engaged in continuous warfare. But this metaphysical dualism, this continuous give and take, can hardly provide hope for a future. Before we agree with such an interpretation, we should remember that we are the church of Jesus Christ. Jesus' final destiny is intimately linked to the destiny that we too will experience as members of his church. The powers of darkness could not confine Christ to death and the grave, and he was raised to a new form of life. Therefore, it is also our hope that the church will not be overcome by the powers of the nether world but will ensue in the glory of God.

The hope of the Old Testament faithful and of the first Christians was centered on the peace of God. This peace of which the liturgy reminds us remains, to this day, the hope of many. In a time of permanent unrest and continuous limited warfare, the peace of God, which God assures, will one day be realized in a new world that stands in stark contrast to our present one. For instance, we read in the Book of Revelation that one day God will dwell in the midst of the people and that all distance, brokenness, and fear will then be overcome (Rev. 21:3–4).

This coming peace of God is anticipated by the church as it lives as a community of those who are reconciled with God and who attempt in an anticipatory way to exercise the office of reconciliation. Reconciliation is something necessary today—in families between the generations, at work between workers and employees, and in politics between one nation and another. Often the church is the only institution that can mediate between two parties when one is no longer willing and able to listen to the other. It was significant for me when a colleague from a theological seminary in China told me that the most important word for the Christians there is neither justification nor liberation but reconciliation. Reconciliation, however, can only radiate from the church if its members are reconciled with God and with one another.

As long as the church itself is torn and fragmented, its testimony to reconciliation does not carry much credibility. The endeavor for unity belongs as an essential part of the church's task of reconciliation. But what has grown separately for several centuries cannot now be made undone within a few years, even if we think that many differences between the churches are now obsolete and no longer divisive. It does not suffice, in an attitude of enlightened indifference, to attempt to bypass our different historical developments. Instead we must be willing to bear one another, to learn from one another, to listen to one another, and to serve the Lord together. The unity of the church is given to us through the confession of one holy catholic church and the communion of saints. If this confession comes alive in us, the church is no longer a relic of the past but a point of orientation in a world that often seems to drift without much orientation. To confess this church and to serve others is not only a big task but also a great opportunity for all those who call themselves Christians.

# 14 | OVERCOMING FEAR

*". . . the forgiveness of sins . . ."*

The quest for a gracious God was the central concern of the Lutheran Reformation. Even so, the Middle Ages had already been largely characterized by the same quest. The crusades, the innumerable donations to the church, and the expansion of monastic life indicate that it was the concern of many people to obtain a gracious God and escape from God's threatening wrath.

This mood of religious fear is understandable when we realize that in the eighteenth century in Europe the average life expectancy was barely thirty-six years. This meant that shortly after one had completed the second decade of life the climax of one's energy and vigor had been reached. Many people did not live to become adults. For instance, in the eighteenth century the French philosopher Jean Jacques Rousseau wrote:

> Though we know approximately the limits of the human life and our chance of attaining that limit, nothing is more uncertain than our life expectancy. Very few obtain old age. The main risks we face are at the beginning of life. The fewer years we have passed by now, the less hope we have that we will live beyond the present. Of all children born, hardly half of them reach adolescence and it is very likely that a student will not live long enough to become a man.

Death was a public fact and had not yet been pushed into the anonymity of sterile clinics. Even in the last century, when many people had large families, almost one third of the children died in infancy.

Even if a person could complete this short life unhampered by calamities, life still contained few pleasures, for instance the celebration of marriage or the dedication of a church. Not only was life short, but it was characterized by drudgery since most human beings lived as the victims of the powers of nature and disease. The vale of toil and tears, known to us through old church hymns, was a reality for these people. Life on earth did not entail any great hopes, and if there was hope at all, so we surmise, it had to come beyond this short life in the hereafter. In order to obtain this future happiness, the desire to assure oneself of God's grace became a central concern because without it the future of a better beyond seemed unattainable. Therefore, the quest for a gracious God corresponded to the desire to make more bearable one's hard life on this earth through the hope for a better beyond.

Since that time our life and the conditions under which we live have changed drastically. The question about a gracious God is hardly raised today because the presuppositions for this question have largely disappeared among us in our affluent society. Certainly we should not lament that change of conditions. Today we can expect a long life; seventy or eighty years are widely accepted as the norm. Hard, physical work, inadequate housing, and the threat of contagious diseases such as the plague—which in the Middle Ages killed the population of entire regions—have become the exceptions. After thousands of years we have finally secured our position here on this earth. We have settled in and attempt to make ourselves at home here. Many things that were considered commonplace generations ago have either disappeared completely or have become superfluous. One of these is the forgiveness of sins. Today to speak of sin is almost a taboo; "sin" is itself a sinful word. We would hardly tell someone in everyday life that he or she is a sinner and has committed a sin.

## HOW SINFUL IS SIN?

Today many are convinced that we should not inject fear in others by making them conscious of their sins. It is commonly believed that by injecting anxiety and guilt feelings we can cause neuroses and other psychic damage. We may still talk about estrangement, but the word "sin" is simply no longer acceptable. Truly, much misuse has been made of the word "sin." Just as we often immediately reject an unacceptable view as liberal or conservative, so in the past any conduct contrary to our own standards was labeled sinful. Sin came to be viewed as being synonymous with taboo. By equating sin with taboo, a concept of sin emerged that smacked of authoritarianism. Also, as more and more taboos collapsed in the course of time, it became more difficult to call something sinful. Perhaps given the biblical understanding of sin, it might not really be so bad after all to understand sin as estrangement.

Roughly speaking, estrangement means that we enter into the wrong terrain. We are no longer where we belong—for example, in our home territory—but somewhere where we are strangers. In this definition sin is characterized as being distant from the place where we actually ought to be. It is as if a trench exists that separates us from others. If we characterize sin as estrangement, however, we must immediately ask ourselves where we ought to be if not in the world in which we have settled. Since we are in this world and indeed want to be there, it would be wrong to characterize this as sinful.

Yet a peculiar change has taken place in our self-understanding. Just as we thought we had mastered this world so that all surprises and insecurities had been conquered, we notice that we have in fact neither mastered this world nor our fellow humans with whom we share it. In contrast to medieval humanity, we need no longer be afraid of the irrational and mysterious. But now it is exactly the rational, the plannable, and the already planned that cause us to fear. We are afraid of an all-out atomic war, of the destruction of the environment, of the depletion of our natural resources; we are simply afraid of the future. In this precarious situation many of us would prefer to start anew so that in a second attempt we might better navigate the dangerous waters in which we find ourselves.

## THE POSSIBILITY OF
## A NEW BEGINNING

Many of us may have dreamed of the possibility of starting life over again. If we look back at our life with satisfaction, we might like to live it over again just because it was so nice. If we are not satisfied with our destiny, then we might prefer to start anew, to learn from the mistakes and the shortcomings of the past in order to make life a little better the second time around. But we all know that these are wishful thoughts. We cannot turn back the hands of time.

The possibility of a new beginning, however, is offered to us through the forgiveness of sins. For instance, Paul wrote to the Christians in Corinth:

> If any one is in Christ, he is a new creation; the old has passed away, behold, the new has come. All this is from God, who through Christ reconciled us to himself and gave us the ministry of reconciliation; that is, in Christ God was reconciling the world to himself, not counting their trespasses against them, and entrusting to us the message of reconciliation (2 Cor. 5:17–19).

When Paul mentions forgiveness or reconciliation here, he does not imply that this will make us into totally new beings. As those who have received forgiveness, we still stand in this world and cannot flee its problems. Our ongoing encounters with other people make us realize that we cannot escape the past.

As Christians we too must admit that forgiving is much easier than forgetting, but our not forgetting often stems from our unwillingness to forget instead of the impossibility of doing so. We are so much a product of the past that we almost feel it is improper to forget something too quickly in order to smooth over something that happened in the past. We are also uncertain whether the same thing might not happen again. Therefore, instead of closing our eyes, we are warned by former events to be on our guard. Yet this mistrust, this living out of the past, also causes a lot of sorrow for us and for others.

If we do not trust someone, then, according to our usual thinking, it is best if we safeguard ourselves by erecting a wall. We go on the defensive and isolate ourselves from others. The solitary existence with which we are confronted today in many places, the uncaring attitude toward neighbors and strangers alike, stems from this distrust and fear. We are uncertain who others really are and what we are getting into. Therefore, the fear of others, the anxiety that what happened to us once may happen again, pushes us ever farther in the direction of isolation and solitary existence. In this situation the realization of forgiveness and reconciliation offers us a totally new understanding of life and effects an openness and a turning to other people.

When we live from the experience of forgiveness, we need not naively assume that everything is just fine. Martin Luther in his Small Catechism instructed us to repent daily and drown the old Adam. Likewise, in the first of his Ninety-five Theses he mentioned that our whole life should be one of continuous repentance. This means that Luther accepted the brokenness of our world as a fact. Even when we live from forgiveness and in openness to others, we will still have new disappointments. Nevertheless, our life is shaped by a totally different approach to this world.

Since we ourselves have experienced that God has turned toward us and that our transgressions are no longer counted, we too are allowed and encouraged to turn with forgiveness to our fellow human beings. Only reconciled people can contribute to reconciliation. When the estrangement of our sinful existence is overcome and we experience that we are at home with God, we no longer need to dig trenches between ourselves and others but instead can share with them our newly found home. How much our quality of life could be improved if politicians and those in public office were ready, in an attitude of reconciliation, to approach each other instead of cutting each other down and telling each other that they are not trustworthy! The same holds true in our own lives.

In our attempts to tame this world and secure the future, we have forgotten that we always live from trust. Our projections about the future of the economy, politics, or our own lives are always based on the trust that the tendencies known to us will not change in an unforeseen way. As we continuously revise our projections, we admit that risk cannot be avoided in relationship to the future. But if we admit that we must maintain openness in this way, why is it so difficult to show the same openness to other people? The saying goes that a burnt child avoids fire. But we cannot totally avoid fire; we need it every day. Can we not learn from this that, our negative experiences of the past notwithstanding, we must still approach other people? The decision for reconciliation with others should be made easier through our experience of reconciliation with God. Luther reminded us that the old Adam is to be drowned in us through daily sorrow and repentance. This means that God does not pardon us only once but rather forgives us every time we ask for pardon and seriously attempt to make a new beginning. Can we be stricter than God?

## TRUST IN GOD'S PRESENCE

The possibility of a new beginning through reconciliation is founded on our trust in God's presence. God does not demand a decision of faith and then disaffectionately measure from a distance whether we have lived up to this decision in all its consequences. Through Jesus Christ we have experienced that God is not a distant God but is close to us. God identifies with the heights and depths of our lives.

The early church thought that God would pardon our sins only once, in baptism, through which they would be undone through the benefits of Christ's death and resurrection. Thus baptism was postponed to the end of life in order that Christians might approach God after death as pure and free of sin as possible. For instance, Emperor Constantine had for many years openly confessed his Christian faith and supported the Christian cause. But only on his deathbed did he allow himself to be baptized to obtain forgiveness of all his sins. Eventually, however, it was recognized that God's guiding, pardoning, and supporting hand is always with us and therefore forgiveness of sins is also possible after baptism.

Because of God's graciousness quite often a certain lightheartedness enters our Christian life. So the French philosopher Voltaire once quipped: "God will forgive because that is his business." Though God is gracious to us, it is dangerous to assume that God will automatically forgive us over and over again. We should not frivolously mistake God's presence as the presence of a buddy. Certainly God is with us also on difficult days. But this love is not so irrational and unhealthy that God simply "closes both eyes." Paul, therefore, repeatedly urges us to take seriously our new beginning with God. In a similar way Jesus stated that a good tree should yield good fruit; otherwise it is not good and will be cut down (Matt. 7:17–18). Our trust in God's presence must be translated into action so that our activity also reflects God's presence. Therefore the forgiveness of sins leads to a manifestation of this new life, which is oriented toward God's presence and derives its strength from it.

Though our life will never be surrounded by a halo since we are bound to our earthly and fragile nature, the experience of God's presence should result in a qualitatively different life style. It is secondary whether we call this new way of life one of sanctification or one of satisfaction. What is important is that others feel something of God's presence through us. If God has become a God who is close at hand, the destructive powers of separation and discord and the fear which underlies them have no place in our life. Jesus therefore reminds us, according to John: "In the world you have tribulation; but be of good cheer, I have overcome the world" (John 16:33).

Though we live in a world characterized by fear and an absence of peace, we need not despair. We can cling to God's presence, which we have experienced in Jesus Christ. He has overcome the world and all its adversity and anxiety. We can trust that this world will not determine our destiny forever. The nearness of God that we experience in the forgiveness of sins points beyond this world to a new one in which God's presence will be made fully manifest. For Christians there is no cause for pessimism about the future or a psychosis of fear. We can trust in the one who has overcome the world and who will lead us to a new future. Forgiveness of sin may sound archaic to some of us but it entails a new beginning and the experience of God's presence. These are essentials if we want to approach a new future. We should thank God ever anew that God offers us this future.

# 15 | HOPE WITHOUT UTOPIA

*". . . the resurrection of the body, and the life everlasting."*

The last passage of the Apostles' Creed witnesses to faith in the resurrection of the dead and in life eternal. When we understand the Holy Spirit as the focus of this third article, then we realize in retrospect that the various points included in this article are an elaboration on the work of the Holy Spirit. The Holy Spirit who works in God's creation is especially manifest in the church. Through the forgiveness of sins, announced in the church, it is possible for us to find our way back to the original unity of humanity. We thereby overcome our estrangement from God and our fellow human beings. As the ultimate consequence of our becoming one with God, we participate in the resurrection of the dead and life eternal. If we make our destiny beyond death wholly dependent on the power of the Holy Spirit, however, we easily could be accused of pious wishful thinking. The reason for this is that this kind of activity of the Holy Spirit can hardly be made intelligible.

## THE DREAM OF ETERNAL LIFE

The dream of eternal life is a basic ingredient of human desire. In almost all religions there exists the belief in life eternal, whether as the entrance into nirvana, the return to a world soul, or the reception into Valhalla. Often this idea is connected with the return to a primal paradisaic state. A golden age will dawn and there will be neither work nor labor, neither sickness nor death. The dream of a thousand years' *Reich*, which was advocated by Friedrich Engels, a collaborator of Karl Marx, and which in the Third Reich of Adolf Hitler came to a sobering but brief attempt at realization, always entails the desire for a new and integral world. For instance, the neo-Marxist Ernst Bloch advocated that in Marxism the tales about the past should be taken seriously and the dream of a golden age should be realized. Only then would the incomplete world be led towards its completion, and only then would we enter where we actually belong, our mother country.

The dream of eternal life is often accompanied by the emergence of messianic figures who promise a new world with paradisaic features. This can lead to the metaphysical embellishment of these figures that we may notice in some socialist countries, but this tendency is also present in younger nations that are still struggling for liberation. That one greets such a leader with "Heil" (i.e., salvation), as happened in Nazi Germany, expresses vividly the desire for a world of wholeness and eternal life.

In Jewish faith, too, the messianic hope, which aims for the establishment of a new kingdom and a new world, was never extinguished. When Israel's national unity collapsed in the Babylonian exile, this intensified for the Jews their germ of hope in the resurrection of the dead. Frequently messianic leaders emerged, although every time this occurred the hope connected with them was disappointed. For instance, a few generations after Jesus' death Bar Kochba was proclaimed as a new messiah. Coins were even minted bearing his name, and some people started to count the years from the beginning of his public activity. The Romans, however, soon put an end to his life and his rebellion. He did not bring about the desired kingdom but instead furthered the collapse of the Jewish state. Thus the disappointed adherers of the "son of the stars," Bar Kochba, changed his name to "son of lie" (Bar Kosiba).

Even the Christian faith has its Messiah. Jesus is called Christ, which means "the anointed one" or "the Messiah." Presumably Jesus was crucified because he made messianic claims, but he disappointed the national political expectations that were commonly connected with such claims. Moreover, in the Christian faith the hope in eternal life is deeply rooted. Would it not follow from the above that we should discard the Christian faith in the future as a dream or as a utopia which does not have sufficient grounding in reality? Who really believes in the resurrection of the dead anyhow?

Such a conclusion would not, however, imply that we have lost interest in life eternal. The immense popularity of the reports of near-death experiences show that many people are eager for "proof" that everything is not over at death. Although we no longer believe in the resurrection of the dead, the feeling continues that we will survive death in some form or other. If we could trace scientifically a continuation of life, as has been attempted in some popular accounts of near-death experiences, we would have assurance beyond death. Then we would know that our brief life does not end but will pass over into a new and beautiful world.

This desire for a completion in the beyond and a continuation of our life is also implied in many prehistoric funeral rites. It was not only a matter of piety that the dead were buried with gifts in their tombs and occasionally even food. It was sensed that existence is not totally over with death and that some preparation ought to be made for the deceased for the life beyond. Yet a dream does not become true just because many believe that it is real. The Christian faith does not condone such dreams but rather confronts the desire for a better beyond with the promise of the resurrection of the dead. In the original Greek text of the Creed, the confession is made that we believe in a resurrection of the "flesh."

## THE PROMISE OF PERSONAL IDENTITY

In the Greek world in which the Christians proclaimed their belief in the resurrection of the dead, the biological and chemical processes through which a corpse decays and is absorbed by nature and integrated into other forms of life were not yet known. But even without this detailed knowledge, the assertion that dead people will be resurrected was an offense even to the slightly educated. Paul experienced this following his speech on the Areopagus in Athens of which we read in Acts 17:22–33. When he told the educated Athenians about the unknown God who had created the world and everything within it, his listeners were attentive. Their response changed quickly once he touched on the theme of the resurrection. We read in Acts: "When they heard of the resurrection of the dead, some mocked; but others said, 'We will hear you again about this'" (Acts 17:32). For the Athenians the idea of eternal life was well known but a resurrection of the dead was unthinkable.

The conditions in Corinth differed only slightly from those in Athens. Otherwise Paul would not have devoted a whole chapter of his letter to the Corinthian congregation to the topic of resurrection. Presumably the Corinthians shook their heads in disbelief as much as the Athenians did when they heard from Paul: "So it is with the resurrection of the dead. What is sown is perishable, what is raised is imperishable. It is sown in dishonor, it is raised in glory. It is sown in weakness, it is raised in power. It is sown a physical body, it is raised a spiritual body" (1 Cor. 15:42–44). We can very well understand the embarrassment of the Corinthians. How should they conceive of a body that will be somehow resurrected by God? Trained in Platonic and Aristotelian thinking they would have found it more logical to consider that something immortal would survive death. Many poets have likewise expressed this idea that something will survive death and that through this one aspect—we may call it soul, or psyche, or the spark of the divine—we will find our unity in God.

The Creed, however, emphasizes the resurrection of the dead or rather that of the flesh. With this claim three items were asserted. Confronted with the dreams of life eternal, it was asserted, first, that there is an actual resurrection and not a fictional one or one in which we merely survive in the memory of God or of posterity. In Greek the word "flesh" was used to show that resurrection is no dream or fiction. Through the emphasis on the resurrection a second point was made: there is no continuation of life beyond death to which we have access through our own being or through our conduct. If there is hope beyond death, it can be grounded only by concluding that the God whom we have experienced graciously in this life will also be gracious to us beyond death. The resurrection of the dead is not a matter of fact but results from God's undeserved grace. God will give us new life beyond death.

Finally, it was asserted that when God raises us to new life, it is God who will give us new and eternal life beyond death. Our personal identity in the new life results from our resurrection from the dead and not through our own eternal nature. This idea of eternal life is to be distinguished from the proposal of Gnosticism, a widespread movement at the beginning of Christianity, in which at death the light sparks contained in each human being are collected and gathered into a world soul. According to this idea, eternal life is composed of one large mosaic in which each individual human being is a tiny building block.

The undifferentiated life after death as proposed by Buddhism is equally alien to the Christian faith. Jesus always emphasized that God loves the individual. We notice this in the parables of the lost sheep, the prodigal son, and the good Samaritan. Though in the Christian faith the individual is connected with and embedded in the community of believers, there is no collective relationship to God. Even so, our faith is also not a private faith that takes place only between us and God. It remains tied to the community of all the saints. Although they are in this community, God addresses individuals. Our identity before God is not lost in death. We need not worry whether we will be resurrected with the same body we now have because, as Paul expressly emphasized, the new body will be of quite different quality. But we are assured that our personal identity, in which we are at home and in which we recognize ourselves, will not be lost.

The question remains, however, whether the faith in the resurrection of the dead is just a wishful dream. What gives this hope more certainty than the many other disappointed hopes in the history of humanity?

## THE REALITY OF THE PROMISE

If we want to determine the degree of reality contained in the promise of the resurrection from the dead, we must do this by considering the one resurrection that has already occurred. In contrast to all the other messianic figures who promised new conditions of life or life eternal, Jesus did not just leave a message. He was, as Paul confessed together with the tradition, "raised on the third day" (1 Cor. 15:4). Jesus was so closely connected with the Spirit of God that neither death nor tomb could hold him forever. This legitimized the claim that he was the Messiah, that is, God's bringer of salvation. When we sing in an anthem, "Salvation unto us has come by God's free grace and favor," this is a confession of Christ's salvational activity, by which he overcame the barriers of death and estrangement that separate us from God. Jesus was not merely a Jewish itinerant preacher with messianic ambition. He was legitimated by God as the Messiah through his resurrection. Therefore we can trust the message in which Jesus claimed that God wants our salvation.

Life eternal is no abstract desire for us but, instead, is inseparably connected with Jesus Christ. Because Jesus Christ was resurrected from the dead, the idea of the resurrection of the dead was endowed with new reality. Jesus Christ was allowed to live after his resurrection in a totally new way of life so that the limiting factors which curtail our present life no longer had power over him. Similarly, we can expect that we too may participate in such a resurrection.

The eternal life that becomes a certainty for us through the destiny of Jesus should not be misunderstood either as a solipsistic, individualized life or as an undifferentiated communal existence. As the Old Testament promises found their fulfillment in Jesus, so this new life must be interpreted on the basis of the Old Testament promises of a continuous and peaceful life in the presence of God. Eternal life is not just a continuous life that is no longer limited by the barriers of aging and perishing; it is permeated by God's eternity. The powers that are hostile to life will no longer have influence on this life. For instance we read in Isaiah that many nations will come to God:

> That he may teach us his ways and that we may walk in his paths. For out of Zion shall go forth the law, and the word of the Lord from Jerusalem. He shall judge between the nations, and shall decide for many peoples; and they shall beat their swords into plowshares, and their spears into pruning hooks; nation shall not lift up sword against nation, neither shall they learn war any more (Isa. 2:3–4).

Not out of fear of punishment but voluntarily, the nations will listen to God and do God's will. God's misused name will be made holy, and unrest will be replaced by peace.

These pictures of the messianic kingdom are alien to us. God's kingdom is so different from our present reality. The images point to something new that no eye has seen and no ear has heard but that we nonetheless deeply desire. What has often been abbreviated to a utopia shall then become reality. When we orient ourselves according to

Jesus Christ our desires for a new life will become real and we may justifiably hope we too will be included on that day.

We have reached the end of our rethinking of the Apostles' Creed. In so doing we have meditated on the basic creed of the Christian church. Many items, however, have not been touched upon nor even mentioned. Yet we may rest assured that God will judge us, not by how much we can believe, but rather by whether we cling to the one who said of himself: "I am the way, and the truth, and the life; no one comes to the Father, but by me" (John 14:6). When we confess Jesus as the Christ, we obtain access to God. But even more, the Creed helps us to understand in a deeper way this basic truth: God has come to us so that we may come to God. We should always be thankful anew that this great God has graciously come down to us insignificant earthlings, and we should praise God for this by shaping our lives ever more closely to Jesus Christ, our example and savior.